OCCASIONAL PAPER **246**

Experience with Large Fiscal Adjustments

George C. Tsibouris, Mark A. Horton, Mark J. Flanagan,
and Wojciech S. Maliszewski

INTERNATIONAL MONETARY FUND
Washington DC
2006

© 2006 International Monetary Fund

Production: IMF Multimedia Services Division
Typesetting: Alicia Etchebarne-Bourdin

Cataloging-in-Publication Data

Experience with large fiscal adjustments/George C. Tsibouris . . . [et al.]—
   Washington, D.C.: International Monetary Fund [2006].

     p. cm.—(Occasional paper; no. 246)

    ISBN 1-58906-458-5
    Includes bibliographical references.

    1. Fiscal policy. 2. Fiscal policy—Case studies. 3. Fiscal policy—
Developing countries. 4. International Monetary Fund. I. Tsibouris, George C.
II. Series: Occasional paper (International Monetary Fund); no. 246.

HJ192.5.E86 2006

recycled paper

Contents

Text Figures

Appendix Tables

Appendix Figures

The following symbols have been used throughout this paper:

. . .   to indicate that data are not available;

—   to indicate that the figure is zero or less than half the final digit shown, or that the item does not exist;

–   between years or months (e.g., 2003–04 or January–June) to indicate the years or months covered, including the beginning and ending years or months;

/   between years (e.g., 2003/04) to indicate a fiscal (financial) year.

"n.a." means not applicable.

"Billion" means a thousand million.

Minor discrepancies between constituent figures and totals are due to rounding.

The term "country," as used in this paper, does not in all cases refer to a territorial entity that is a state as understood by international law and practice; the term also covers some territorial entities that are not states, but for which statistical data are maintained and provided internationally on a separate and independent basis.

Preface

This Occasional Paper analyzes the experience of countries that have implemented very sizable fiscal adjustments over the past three decades. It aims to identify key conditions and institutional approaches that have contributed to sustained outcomes and to favorable macroeconomic developments. In this way, the paper may provide operational guidance to policymakers. The paper was prepared by George Tsibouris, Mark Horton, Mark Flanagan, and Wojciech Maliszewski while they were in the IMF's Fiscal Affairs Department (FAD).

The authors would like to thank Teresa Ter-Minassian, Jeff Davis, Sanjeev Gupta, and Rolando Ossowski for their guidance and advice on this study. Useful comments and suggestions were also provided by Anupam Basu, Adrienne Cheasty, Alfredo Cuevas, James Daniel, Xavier Debrun, Liam Ebrill, Hans Flickenschild, Manal Fouad, Michael Keen, Steven Symansky, and Ricardo Velloso. We are also grateful for feedback provided by participants in the annual FAD Academic Panel Conference in January 2004. Case studies were prepared by Thomas Baunsgaard, Ana Corbacho, Stephan Danninger, Lubin Doe, Stefano Fassina, Mark Flanagan, Mark Horton, and Antonio Spilimbergo. Luis Blancas and Noel Perez Benitez provided excellent research assistance throughout, while Anna Mateos-Perry and Juliet Narsiah ably assisted in preparing the manuscript. Archana Kumar of the External Relations Department edited the manuscript and coordinated production of the publication.

Opinions expressed in this paper are solely those of its authors and do not necessarily reflect the views of the International Monetary Fund, its Executive Directors, or national authorities.

I Overview

There are instances when policymakers may have little option but to consider a sizable fiscal adjustment. In such circumstances, they may be confronted with questions such as, Can a large fiscal adjustment be implemented successfully? How is a large adjustment best designed and implemented? What will be its impact on the economy?

This paper sheds light on these questions by describing the experience of countries that have undertaken large fiscal adjustments over the past three decades. It identifies preconditions, common policy approaches, and institutional arrangements underlying successful and unsuccessful adjustment episodes, thereby providing operational guidance to policymakers.

The key findings of this paper are the following:

- Large adjustments have occurred relatively frequently over the past 30 years. Some 300 episodes of consolidation in excess of 5 percent of GDP were identified over the past three decades, nearly half of which involved an adjustment over a relatively short time span of just one to two years. Sizable consolidations have been implemented under a range of circumstances, including during financial crises, as part of planned adjustments, and in connection with improved economic circumstances. Large adjustments have been undertaken by a diverse group of countries, including G-7 countries, EU member states, resource-rich countries, major emerging market countries, and numerous developing countries.

- Macroeconomic conditions at the outset of large fiscal adjustments were relatively difficult. Countries that undertook large adjustments had significantly higher debt ratios and inflation at the outset, as well as more sluggish growth of GDP, private consumption, and investment, relative to countries that undertook small fiscal consolidations. Restoring sustainability and ensuring access to short-term financing proved to be pressing needs. The structure of the fiscal accounts for countries that undertook large fiscal adjustments showed greater reliance on relatively volatile

grants and nontax revenues, less reliance on domestic indirect taxes, and more capital investment outlays in the run-up to the adjustment.

- Durable large fiscal adjustments relied primarily on expenditure reduction. Statistical and econometric analyses suggest that a balanced reduction of capital and current spending, with an emphasis on a durable lowering of the wage bill, worked best in these situations. A high interest burden proved relatively difficult to overcome and led to a lower incidence of success. Medium-term budgetary frameworks tangibly supported the adjustment by providing a road map and a benchmark when additional measures were needed.

- There were also cases of durable fiscal adjustments based on revenue enhancement, particularly in countries with low initial revenue-to-GDP ratios and where the pace of adjustment was more gradual. This allowed for sustained implementation over time of tax policy and administration reforms.

- High political risk had an adverse impact on the duration of adjustment. Case studies confirm that political support was a key element in sustained fiscal adjustments.

- Large adjustments, in contrast with small consolidations, generally had a positive macroeconomic impact. Among large adjustments, a more gradual pace of implementation seems to have led to more favorable macroeconomic outcomes.

The analysis of individual country experiences also highlights the importance of fiscal structural reforms. In particular,

- greater transparency and improved monitoring of the fiscal stance has helped to focus attention on underlying policies at an early stage and to generate stronger political support;

- enhanced legal and institutional arrangements, as well as fiscal indicators such as the nonresource balance in oil-producing countries, have played an important role; and

- countries with more advanced expenditure management systems faced a less arduous task when undertaking fiscal adjustments by being able to better track and control contingent liabilities and tax expenditures, and to improve debt management.

II Introduction

This Occasional Paper describes the experience of countries that have undertaken large fiscal adjustments over the past three decades. It identifies preconditions, common policy approaches, and institutional arrangements underlying successful and unsuccessful adjustment episodes, in order to provide operational guidance for policymakers. It aims to address the following questions:

- Can a large fiscal adjustment be implemented successfully?

- How is a large adjustment best designed and implemented? and

- What will be the impact of a large fiscal adjustment on the economy?

This paper extends earlier studies of fiscal adjustment by focusing on particularly large adjustments and by examining a much wider sample of countries than was previously done. Statistical comparisons, duration analysis, and event study techniques are applied to a data set of 165 countries over 30 years to assess the effects of adjustment design and staging on the sustainability of fiscal consolidation and on resulting macroeconomic outcomes. This paper also incorporates the findings of 13 case studies, covering a range of industrial, emerging market, transition, primary resource–producing, and developing countries, to provide further insight into the motivation, design, and implementation of sizable fiscal consolidations.

It is organized as follows. Section III elaborates the definition of a large fiscal adjustment that is used in the paper, describes the data set on adjustment episodes, and compares and contrasts the characteristics of large fiscal adjustments relative to smaller consolidations. Section IV reviews factors that contributed to the durability of large fiscal adjustments. Section V assesses the macroeconomic outcomes of consolidation episodes. Section VI provides some concluding remarks.

III What Is a "Large" Fiscal Adjustment?

In this study, an episode of fiscal adjustment is defined as any year or succession of years of uninterrupted improvement in the fiscal primary balance. Data were assembled for the 165 countries, covering the period 1971–2001. Reflecting availability and the need for comparability, the fiscal data cover the consolidated central government, primarily on a cash basis. To limit the influence of exogenous events, adjustment episodes of oil exporters were excluded for periods of significant upward changes in real oil prices.

The frequency and diversity of sizable fiscal adjustments during 1971–2001 is noteworthy (Table 3.1).[1] For example, there have been some 300 episodes of fiscal consolidation in excess of 5 percent of GDP over the past three decades. At the same time, there were 118 adjustment episodes that involved consolidation equivalent to or greater than 30 percent of government expenditures. One also finds significant diversity in the length and pace of adjustment episodes: 38 adjustment episodes exceeded five years in length, and over two-thirds of the total consolidation was concentrated in the first year for the majority of countries in the sample. Box 3.1 discusses possible explanations for the relative frequency of sizable adjustments.

A number of considerations went into developing a definition of what constitutes a "large" fiscal adjustment. Given the rather diverse sample of countries, this paper looks at two criteria: the size of the adjustment as a share of GDP and as a share of government expenditures. What may seem to be a modest consolidation relative to GDP for some countries may be exceptionally large for a country with a small government. In other studies, the definition has tended to be based on specific thresholds in terms of GDP and size of government, above which episodes would be considered "large";[2] however,

this approach tends to be somewhat arbitrary. Instead, this paper defines as large those fiscal adjustments that fall into the top one-third of all adjustment episodes, both as a share of GDP and as a share of government expenditures. This corresponds to thresholds of 6.3 percent of GDP and 21.8 percent of the initial size of government expenditures beyond which an adjustment is considered "large."

This approach identified 155 large adjustment episodes. Among these, 63 were "front-loaded" cases, in which more than two-thirds of the overall adjustment took place in the first year, while 55 were "gradual" cases, in which one-third or less of the consolidation took place in the first year. This statistical methodology does not allow for a distinction between policy-induced and endogenous adjustments, though the magnitudes in question would suggest that the former would account for the majority of the adjustment.[3]

Are large adjustments sufficiently different from smaller consolidations to warrant a separate study? For comparison, 154 smaller episodes were also identified. These belonged to the lower one-third of both marginal distributions, where the size of the adjustment was less than 3 percent of GDP and 15 percent of the initial size of government. Initial macroeconomic and fiscal conditions suggest that the sample of large adjustments is indeed distinct from the sample of smaller consolidations:

- Large adjustments were initiated under more difficult macroeconomic circumstances than smaller adjustments. Inflation in the period leading up to adjustment episodes was higher, on average, while growth of GDP, private consumption, and private investment were lower, when compared with countries that initiated small adjustments (Table 3.2).

- Restoring sustainability and ensuring access to short-term financing were more pressing issues for large adjusters. The ratio of public debt to

---

[1]Appendix I elaborates on these definitions and discusses their limitations in more detail. See Tables A1.1 and A1.2 for country coverage of the data set and Table A2.1 for a full list of the large adjustment episodes.

[2]See Alesina and Perotti (1996); and Alesina and Ardagna (1998).

[3]The use of cyclically adjusted measures did not prove feasible, because of data limitations.

Table 3.1. Episodes of Fiscal Adjustment by Size and Length, 1971–2001[1]
(Excluding oil-producing countries)[2]

	Number	Adjustment by Size of Government[3]					Length of Adjustment		Initial Adjustment[4]	
		0%–<6%	6%–<18%	18%–<30%	30%–<42%	>42%	≤2 years	≥5 years	≤1/3 of total	>2/3 of total
I. Total adjustment episodes	902	240	361	183	74	44	720	38	173	590
of which: initial adjustment <0.5% GDP	145									
By adjustment size (in percent of GDP)										
0%–<1%	163	158	5	0	0	0	162	1	3	153
1%–<3%	279	81	183	15	0	0	246	1	39	206
3%–<5%	160	1	113	39	6	1	128	2	32	96
5%–<7%	113	0	38	55	16	4	77	10	36	52
7%–<9%	72	0	17	41	8	6	45	6	21	32
≥9%	115	0	5	33	44	33	62	18	42	51
of which: >5% of GDP	300									
>30% of initial government size	118									
>5% of GDP, with 2/3 of adjustment up front	135									
II. Total episodes, excluding OECD countries	749	170	300	167	69	43	611	18	128	500
of which: initial adjustment <0.5% GDP	106									
By adjustment size (in percent of GDP)										
0%–<1%	124	119	5	0	0	0	123	1	2	118
1%–<3%	229	51	163	15	0	0	204	0	29	172
3%–<5%	139	0	94	38	6	1	114	1	25	86
5%–<7%	94	0	25	50	15	4	69	2	25	47
7%–<9%	61	0	10	37	8	6	41	3	15	28
≥9%	102	0	3	27	40	32	60	11	32	49
of which: >5% of GDP	257									
>30% of initial government size	112									
>5% of GDP, with 2/3 of adjustment up front	124									

Sources: IMF, *Government Finance Statistics* (various issues); and IMF staff estimates.
[1] An episode of fiscal adjustment is defined as a period of continuous improvement of the primary balance of the consolidated central government.
[2] For countries with oil exports in excess of 25 percent of GDP, during any five-year period and for adjustments that took place during 1973, 1979–80, and 1999–2000.
[3] In percent of consolidated central government expenditures in the year prior to commencement of adjustment.
[4] Extent of consolidation undertaken in the first year, as a share of the total adjustment during the episode.

Box 3.1. Frequency of Large Fiscal Adjustments

Why have sizable fiscal adjustments taken place frequently over the past three decades? The factors that underlie a sustainable fiscal position are subject to abrupt and frequent change, creating the need for large fiscal adjustment.

- Primary balances may shift rapidly due to exogenous factors. Revenues may deteriorate due to movements in key commodity prices or to a sudden deterioration in tax administration (Philippines, 1998–2002). Expenditure requirements may also change quickly, as they did in Russia when the need to address the social costs of transition intensified in 1994, or in Lebanon with the need for extensive postwar reconstruction outlays in the 1990s.

- Real interest rate shocks may result from global policy shifts (disinflation in industrial countries during the early 1980s) or contagion (during the Asian crisis). Even countries without access to global capital markets may face real interest rate shocks due to the volatility of aid flows.

- Growth prospects may be altered significantly by sudden shocks in trade patterns, as happened in Finland in 1991–92 with the collapse of the Soviet Union, and in Lithuania in 1998 with the financial crisis in Russia. Prospects may also be dimmed by the outbreak of war or civil unrest and long-lasting effects on the quality of institutions vital for growth.

- Public debt may increase suddenly if contingent liabilities accrue and are called. There are a number of examples in the past decade of fiscal adjustments in response to a sudden sharp increase in public debt related to banking crises, including in Finland (1991–92), Indonesia (1998–99), Jamaica (1996–98), and Turkey (2001).

Although sudden macro-fiscal developments may dictate a sudden need for a sizable consolidation, the availability of financing may also play an important role in determining when the adjustment will be undertaken. Financial markets, bilateral donors, or international financial institutions may be willing to provide support only on the basis of policy actions or on the assumption (sometimes mistaken) that shocks are temporary. Sudden shifts in sentiment may then abruptly alter the availability of financing and leave little choice but to undertake a large fiscal contraction or face default.

A separate literature examines the conditions under which a fiscal and/or debt crisis may emerge and the variables that help in predicting such events (see Hemming, Kell, and Schimmelpfennig, 2003).

Table 3.2. Pre-Adjustment Macroeconomic Context[1]

	Full Sample	Large Adjustments	Small Adjustments
Number of episodes	657	155	154
Real GDP growth one year prior to adjustment[2]	3.0	2.1*	3.8
CPI inflation one year prior to adjustment[2]	15.6	19.7**	10.8
Trade balance one year prior to adjustment[2, 3]	–8.6	–8.0	–8.4
Real consumption growth one year prior to adjustment[2]	3.3	0.2**	4.8
Real investment growth one year prior to adjustment[2]	6.0	0.2	5.4

Sources: IMF, *Global Financial Statistics* (various issues); and IMF staff estimates.

* Significant at 5 percent level.

** Significant at 1 percent level.

[1] Large adjustments are defined as greater than 6.3 percent of GDP and 21.8 percent of initial government expenditures. Small adjustments are episodes in which consolidation was less than 3 percent of GDP and 15 percent of government size.

[2] Simple average for all cases of adjustment.

[3] In percent of GDP.

GDP was twice as large, on average, in the large adjustment episodes than in the smaller ones, and the average primary deficit in the year prior to initiation of adjustment was four times as great (Table 3.3). Moreover, financing requirements increased sharply in the period prior to adjustment.

- Countries that initiated large adjustments had a greater degree of revenue risk and more expenditure flexibility (Table 3.4). On average, in the large adjustment episodes, there was a greater reliance on more volatile grants and nontax revenues, less reliance on domestic indirect taxes,

Table 3.3. Pre-Adjustment Financing Context
(In percent of GDP, unless otherwise indicated)

	Full Sample	Large Adjustments	Small Adjustments
Number of episodes	657	155	154
Average primary balance in the year prior to adjustment	−5.7	−10.0*	−2.5
Average debt stabilizing (t−1) primary balance[1]	−0.9	−0.2	−1.5
Sustainability gap	−4.8	−9.7	−0.9
Average public debt in the year prior to adjustment	69.7	84.7*	41.3
Change in recourse to external financing[2]	0.7	1.3*	0.4
Change in recourse to domestic financing[2]	2.1	3.5	0.7

Sources: IMF, *Government Finance Statistics* (various issues); and IMF staff estimates.

* Significant at 1 percent level.

[1]Calculated on the basis of debt service and CPI inflation to derive real interest rates.

[2]Increase in financing in the year prior to initiating adjustment.

Table 3.4. Pre-Adjustment Budget Structure
(In percent of total revenues and grants and total primary expenditures)[1]

	Full Sample[2]		Large Adjustments	Small Adjustments
Number of episodes	657		155	154
Total revenues and grants	100.0		100.0	100.0
Tax revenues, *of which:*	74.8	(7.5)	69.5**	78.9
Taxes on income, profits, and capital gains, *of which:*	21.8	(5.4)	22.4	22.4
Individual	11.6		11.4	12.3
Corporate	10.7		11.8	10.9
Taxes on payroll	0.5		0.6	0.5
Taxes on property	1.4		1.2	1.7
Domestic taxes on goods and services, *of which:*	24.6	(6.1)	21.4**	26.8
General taxes, turnover, VAT	13.9		13.4	14.6
Excises	10.1		8.9	10.5
Taxes on international trade and transactions, *of which:*	18.3	(6.5)	18.8	18.3
Import duties	16.0		16.0	16.4
Export duties	2.0		1.8	1.8
Other taxes	1.9		1.7	1.6
Nontax revenues	17.3	(6.2)	21.0**	14.4
Capital revenues	0.6		0.8	0.6
Grants	7.9	(6.1)	9.5*	6.7
Unclassified revenues	0.3		0.2	0.2
Total primary expenditure	100.0		100.0	100.0
Primary current expenditure, *of which:*	70.7	(8.9)	67.6**	72.9
Subsidies	22.9	(7.2)	20.9*	25.0
Goods and services (excluding wages)	19.6	(7.6)	20.2	20.5
Wages	25.4	(7.3)	24.5	25.2
Unclassified current expenditure	2.7		2.0	2.1
Capital	24.2	(7.7)	26.8*	22.5
Net lending	5.1	(5.2)	5.6	4.6
Unclassified expenditure	0.9		0.5	2.0

Sources: IMF, *Government Finance Statistics* (various issues); and IMF staff estimates.

* Significant at the 5 percent level.

** Significant at the 1 percent level.

[1]Simple average for sample of countries in the year prior to commencing adjustment.

[2]Numbers in parentheses are the pooled standard deviations for the entire sample.

and a greater share of outlays was devoted to capital spending.

The 13 case studies provide further insight and details on the motivation, design, implementation, and outcome of large adjustments. In all of the cases, difficult macroeconomic conditions prevailed, including a sharp contraction of output and high rates of inflation. Stemming a sharp rise in public debt was a key motivation for the adjustment in several of these countries. Appendix III provides more details on these case studies.

IV What Sustains a Large Fiscal Adjustment?

Three techniques were used to shed light on the factors underlying sustained large fiscal adjustments. First, following Alesina and Perotti (1996), separate samples of successful and unsuccessful adjustment episodes were identified to highlight key changes in the structure of revenues and expenditures that took place in successful or sustained cases. In addition, insights about tax and expenditure policy measures that worked—and those that did not—were provided by the case studies. Finally, econometric analysis was used to formally examine broader questions of adjustment and to identify the influence of macroeconomic, political, and institutional factors.

Statistical Analysis and Case Study Findings

Comparing the design of sustained adjustment episodes with those that were reversed helps to illustrate the role of fiscal policy choices in sustaining adjustment. Successful adjustments were defined as episodes in which reversals were less than one-fifth of the total adjustment.[4] From the 155 large adjustment episodes identified earlier, 66 were sustained. Of these, 28 were "front-loaded" and 21 were "gradual." For comparison, 25 reversed adjustments, where more than 60 percent of the total adjustment was not maintained, were identified.

Sustained adjustment episodes have tended to rely mainly on spending reductions (Table 4.1). Expenditure cuts constituted three-quarters of the total effort in sustained large adjustments, focusing on current spending and, in particular, on subsidies and wages. This result is consistent with earlier studies. Expenditure measures that focus on the wage bill, subsidies, and transfers may also lead to positive effects on the labor market and competitiveness. By contrast, reversed adjustments placed more weight on revenue gains, particularly from taxes on international trade, which may reflect favorable, but transitory, commodity price or exchange rate developments.

The case studies help provide information on the types of expenditure measures used to effect sustained adjustments. Five of the six case studies that can be classified as expenditure-based adjustments were sustained (Tables 4.2, A3.2, and A3.3).

- Among these case studies, expenditure measures tended to be spread across multiple spending categories and agencies, although sizable cuts in the wage bill took place. These were effected, for example, by freezes in hiring and pay in Canada, and nominal pay cuts in Lithuania.[5] In South Africa, a reduction of the wage bill was targeted over several years, allowing for savings through attrition and severance, redeployment, and moderate nominal wage increases. Brazil made efforts to contain personnel and administration outlays at all levels of government. Substantial cuts in subsidies or lending to enterprises were also put in place after functional spending reviews in Canada, Lithuania, and New Zealand. Transfers to lower levels of government were reduced in Canada and Finland, while improved expenditure management helped strengthen finances at the provincial level in South Africa.

- Although pension and unemployment schemes were cut back in some countries, social spending was increased in others, including in Brazil, where entitlement spending increased after 1999; in New Zealand, where social assistance rose by nearly 4 percent of GDP during the adjustment; and in South Africa, where social spending was redirected to the poor. Several of the more institutionally advanced countries established medium-term expenditure frameworks, which helped governments set and meet multiyear priorities and build credibility (Canada, Lithuania, New Zealand, and South Africa). Box 4.1 provides information on these and other structural fiscal reforms.

---

[4]More specifically, a reversal of the initial adjustment over the first three post-adjustment years.

[5]Wage restraint also played a key role in Côte d'Ivoire, which implemented a revenue-based adjustment. In other countries, however, pay freezes were linked to subsequent ad hoc wage increases, underscoring the importance of medium-term planning frameworks.

Table 4.1. Components of Sustained Versus Reversed Fiscal Adjustments
(In percent of the contribution to change in primary balance)

	Large Adjustments	Small Reversal[1]	Large Reversal[2]
Number of episodes	155	66	25
Primary balance	100.0	100.0	100.0
Total revenues and grants	30.0	24.4**	49.9
Tax revenues, *of which:*	17.3	13.7*	25.9
Taxes on income, profits, and capital gains, *of which:*	6.9	4.6	10.2
Individual	1.9	0.3	4.1
Corporate	4.1	3.9	5.1
Taxes on payroll	0.3	0.5	−0.1
Taxes on property	0.2	0.5	−1.8
Domestic taxes on goods and services, *of which:*	5.9	6.1	5.0
General taxes, turnover, VAT	5.1	4.5	7.3
Excises	1.2	1.1	1.1
Taxes on international trade and transactions, *of which:*	0.4	2.4**	10.8
Import duties	0.9	0.5	2.9
Export duties	2.1	0.5	7.9
Other taxes	0.4	1.1	−1.0
Nontax revenues	7.9	4.8	15.8
Capital revenues	0.6	0.2	2.9
Grants	4.8	5.9	8.1
Unclassified revenues	1.1	2.2	0.1
Total primary expenditure	70.0	75.6**	50.1
Primary current expenditure, *of which:*	31.0	36.4**	16.4
Subsidies	14.9	18.6*	6.8
Goods and services (excluding wages)	8.9	10.7	10.5
Wages	7.6	9.4*	−0.2
Unclassified current expenditure	−0.5	−2.4	−0.7
Capital	25.0	27.5	14.7
Net lending	13.9	11.7	19.0
Unclassified expenditure	3.7	5.5	1.4

Sources: IMF, *Government Finance Statistics* (various issues); and IMF staff estimates.

Note: VAT = value-added tax.

* Significant at the 10 percent level.

** Significant at the 5 percent level.

[1]Episodes in which the primary balance continually improved with no reversal in the first three post-adjustment years, or where reversal was limited, on average to 20 percent of the total adjustment.

[2]Episodes in which at least 60 percent of the total adjustment was reversed.

Although expenditure-based consolidations appear to be more likely to be sustained, there were conditions under which revenue-based adjustments were successful. Countries with relatively low initial revenue-to-GDP ratios were more likely to have based their adjustment on revenue gains. They were also more likely to have seen their adjustment be sustained as compared with countries with higher revenue-to-GDP ratios. Splitting the sample of 155 large adjustments between countries with revenues of less than 25 percent of GDP in the initial year and those above this threshold indicates that 8 out of 20 countries that pursued a revenue-based adjustment starting from a low ratio saw the adjustment endure (Table 4.3). By contrast, just 1 out of 11 cases of revenue-based adjustment among high-revenue countries was sustained. This finding is consistent with earlier studies.[6] However, even for countries with low initial revenue ratios, the expenditure strategy appears to offer a greater likelihood of effecting an enduring change on the fiscal position: 59 percent versus 40 percent.

The case studies provide additional insight into the success of revenue measures. These tended to aim at broadening income tax bases and were

[6]See, for example, Abed and others (1998); and Gupta and others (2005).

Table 4.2. Success of Fiscal Adjustment in Case Studies

Case	Success	Adjustment Design	Adjustment Execution	Staging	Revenue Measures	Expenditure Measures
Brazil 1999–2003	Sustained	Revenues	Revenues with some expenditure measures	Up-front	Increases in taxes on turnover, financial intermediation, petroleum products; increase in the state-level VAT.	Efforts to contain personnel and administration expenditures at all levels of government; public investment cuts.
Canada 1999–2003	Sustained	Expenditures	Expenditures with tax reforms	Gradual	PIT and CIT base broadening and rate reductions; increased excises.	Cuts in subsidies, defense, and wage bill; lower intergovernmental transfers, with subnational revenue and spending measures.
Côte d'Ivoire 1993–2000	Sustained (adjustment in early years)	Revenues	Mixed, durability due to expenditure restraint	Up-front	Trade tax gains with depreciation; rationalization of VAT.	Wage restraint; lower interest payments with reduced debt stock.
Finland 1992–2000	Sustained	Expenditures	Mixed	Gradual	PIT and CIT base broadening and rate reductions; introduction of VAT.	Cuts in transfers to other levels of government (with revenue-raising measures at local levels); cuts in subsidies and wage bill.
Jamaica 1998–2001	Unsustained	Revenues	Mixed	Up-front	Numerous tax increases and adjustments (e.g., VAT, interest withholding).	Cuts in capital investment and goods and services.
Lebanon 1998–2002	Mixed; large debt burden continued to increase	Expenditures	Expenditures; introduction of VAT	Up-front	Introduction of VAT.	Cuts in capital spending; few significant reforms in civil service, social programs, or expenditure management.
Lithuania 1999–2003	Sustained	Expenditures	Expenditures	Up-front	Payroll tax increase unsuccessful; increased excises; lower CIT rate; increase of PIT nontax minimum.	Suspension of savings restitution payments; reduced budgetary lending to companies; wage restraint; cuts in goods and services and capital spending.
New Zealand 1983–88	Sustained	Expenditures	Mixed	Gradual	PIT and CIT base broadening and rate reductions; VAT introduction.	Cuts in industrial and agricultural subsidies, net lending.
Nigeria 1990–2000	Unsustained	Revenues	Revenues	Up-front	Introduction of VAT and higher oil prices.	Unsustained wage compression (1995–97); increased spending from 1999 constitutional reforms.
Russia 1995–98	Unsustained	Revenues	Expenditures, with buildup of arrears	Up-front	Revenue performance poor through adjustment.	Cuts in transfers, subsidies, defense spending, and public investment.
Russia 1999–2002	Sustained	Mixed	Mixed	Up-front	Improved oil taxation; centralization of taxes.	Strengthened expenditure control.

Table 4.2 (concluded)

Case	Success	Adjustment Design	Adjustment Execution	Staging	Revenue Measures	Expenditure Measures
South Africa 1993–2001	Sustained	Expenditures	Largely expenditure-based; revenue-neutral tax reforms	Gradual	Higher VAT; PIT reforms; capital gains tax introduction; improved taxation of mining and financial sectors.	Wage restraint; cuts in defense spending, subsidies, and capital investment; reorientation of spending to social categories.
Zambia 1989–94	Unsustained	Revenues	Revenues	Up-front	Import taxes; receipts from SOEs (dividends, tax arrears).	Recourse to expenditure arrears; little progress on key expenditure reforms.

Sources: Country authorities; IMF staff reports.

Note: PIT = personal income tax; CIT = corporate income tax; VAT = value-added tax; SOE= state-owned enterprise.

undertaken in countries with more sophisticated revenue administrations and longer periods of implementation (Brazil, Canada, Finland, New Zealand, and South Africa).[7] Gains from the introduction of value-added taxes (VAT) in Lebanon and Nigeria, and from VAT harmonization in Côte d'Ivoire (in accordance with the tax reforms of the West African Economic Union), were also sustained, likely reflecting the relatively universal initial coverage of these taxes and the incentive to comply in order to receive credits and refunds. In contrast, unsuccessful approaches were characterized by dependence on relatively narrow tax bases and weak administrations. Tax measures in Jamaica, Nigeria, Russia, and Zambia (1995–98) were focused on higher fees and excise taxes, particularly on fuels, and appear to have been relatively easy to evade. Higher taxes on commodities were also prone to evasion and volatility. Currency depreciation boosted revenue gains for a period of time in Côte d'Ivoire and Russia (1998–2002). The Russian adjustment effort in 1999–2002 benefited from higher oil prices and a change in the political environment that allowed for strengthened taxation of the oil and gas sectors.

Different adjustment strategies may be feasible, depending on the desired pace of adjustment (Table 4.4). The degree to which up-front and gradual approaches were sustained was broadly similar, but enduring up-front cases placed more emphasis on revenues than did the gradual cases, particularly trade taxes and nontax revenues.[8] Sustained gradual adjustments relied to a greater extent on cuts on primary current spending, especially wages.

To assess whether initial macroeconomic and fiscal conditions placed constraints on adjustment design, cases of "forced" and "discretionary" adjustment were identified from among the 155 episodes. Specifically, "forced" adjustments were defined as having a significant solvency problem (as indicated by a large gap between the actual and sustainable primary balances) and a growing liquidity problem (as indicated by a marked increase in domestic financing prior to the initiation of adjustment). "Discretionary" adjustments were defined conversely. Separating the samples by looking at the top and bottom third of the relevant statistical distributions, 20 forced adjustments and 21 discretionary adjustments were identified. These samples were almost identical in terms of their length and phasing of adjustment. Forced episodes were not as successful as discretionary ones at achieving a sustainable primary balance by the end of the adjustment phase, but they were more successful at making a large proportion of the adjustment endure, consistent with their circumstance.

Initial conditions do serve as a guide to adjustment design. Forced adjustments are almost wholly (i.e., 88 percent of the time) based on expenditure cuts, whether the adjustment is sustained or not (Table 4.5). In contrast, for cases where there is less concern about solvency and greater discretion about the adjustment, the approach tends to be more balanced, relying approximately equally on revenue and expenditure measures. Severe fiscal stress appears to be associated with severe macroeconomic stress, so that revenue measures may prove to be ineffective in the midst of a sharp decline of private activity. With limited financing available, expenditure cuts may offer the clearest prospect for restor-

---

[7]See Table A3.3.

[8]Previous studies have noted that the reliance on nontax revenues may reflect changes in accounting treatment or one-time transactions.

Box 4.1. Case Studies: Structural Fiscal Reforms

In nearly all of the country case studies, structural fiscal reforms supported consolidation.

- Reforms to budgeting, such as the introduction of medium-term fiscal policy frameworks and organic budget laws, were implemented in Brazil, Canada, Finland, Lithuania, New Zealand, and South Africa. In Brazil, several constitutional provisions, as well as the Fiscal Responsibility Law, helped support the development, implementation, and monitoring of the budget process. Expenditure management and treasury operations were strengthened in Lebanon, Lithuania, Russia, and South Africa. While arrears undermined the first adjustment in Russia, improved expenditure management supported the second consolidation.

- Tax reforms were introduced in most countries. Canada, Finland, and New Zealand reduced personal and corporate tax rates, eliminated exemptions, and taxed previously nontaxed income sources. A similar approach taken in South Africa was guided by an early tax reform blueprint prepared by an expert commission. Lebanon and Nigeria introduced value-added taxes, and Russia improved oil company taxation.

- Several countries strengthened tax administration. South Africa unified its tax and customs administrations; improved wages; and upgraded computerization, risk management, and taxpayer services. Zambia also established a consolidated tax administration agency, and Côte d'Ivoire established a large taxpayer unit. Tax administration improvements were also pursued in Russia and Lebanon.

- Adjustment by subnational governments and improved intergovernmental fiscal arrangements sustained consolidation in Canada, Finland, Russia, and South Africa. The measures included clearer revenue assignments and transfer rules in South Africa, establishment of expenditure norms and formulas for mandated spending in Lithuania, introduction of block grants with equalization mechanisms in Finland, and enactment of subnational borrowing rules and limits in Canada. Successful efforts to strengthen subnational expenditure control were a key element of the second adjustment in Russia.

Additional information can be found in Appendix Table A3.4.

Table 4.3. Initial Conditions and Fiscal Adjustment

Initial Revenue Ratio[1]	Adjustment Approach	Cases		Success Rate (in percent)
		Total	Enduring	
<25 percent of GDP	Revenue-based	20	8	40
	Mixed	10	2	20
	Expenditure-based	46	27	59
	Total	76	37	49
>25 percent of GDP	Revenue-based	11	1	9
	Mixed	17	9	53
	Expenditure-based	51	19	37
	Total	79	29	37

Sources: IMF, *Government Finance Statistics*; and IMF staff estimates.
[1]In the year prior to the initiation of fiscal adjustment.

ing sustainability. The difficult economic and, frequently, political circumstances under which forced adjustments take place may also act to curtail opposition to difficult measures, particularly in terms of cuts in spending programs that are targeted to specific constituencies.

Among the case studies, the forced adjustment scenario can be showcased by the experience of Lithuania. As output declined sharply in 1999 and early 2000, large fiscal and external current account deficits raised concerns not about solvency, but about the sustainability of the country's currency board arrangement. Although payroll taxes were increased in the 2000 budget, yields declined as unemployment rose, necessitating further spending cuts to build credibility and support the currency board.

Table 4.4. Enduring Adjustments: Up-Front Versus Gradual Cases
(In percent of the contribution to change in primary balance)

	Small Reversal[1]	Of Which:	
		Up-front	Gradual
Number of adjustment episodes	66	28	21
Primary balance	100.0	100.0	100.0
Total revenues and grants	24.4	26.4	14.1
Tax revenues, *of which:*	13.7	12.4	13.1
Taxes on income, profits, and capital gains, *of which:*	4.6	4.9	1.9
Individual	0.3	0.5	−0.9
Corporate	3.9	5.9	0.5
Taxes on payroll	0.5	0.2	0.5
Taxes on property	0.5	0.5	0.5
Domestic taxes on goods and services, *of which:*	6.1	6.7	7.7
General taxes, turnover, VAT	4.5	4.6	5.1
Excises	1.1	1.1	0.8
Taxes on international trade and transactions, *of which:*	2.4	4.0*	−1.5
Import duties	0.5	1.1	−1.6
Export duties	0.5	1.0	−0.4
Other taxes	1.1	0.7	1.3
Nontax revenues	4.8	13.5*	−6.2
Capital revenues	0.2	0.6	−1.6
Grants	5.9	0.5	7.2
Unclassified revenues	2.2	3.8	1.6
Total primary expenditure	75.6	73.6	85.9
Primary current expenditure, *of which:*	36.4	30.3	43.8
Subsidies	18.6	14.7	22.0
Goods and services (excluding wages)	10.7	10.6	12.2
Wages	9.4	6.8*	16.7
Unclassified current expenditure	−2.4	−1.9	−7.1
Capital	27.5	34.6	29.1
Net lending	11.7	8.7	13.0
Unclassified expenditure	5.5	9.8	2.5

Sources: IMF, *Government Finance Statistics* (various issues); and IMF staff estimates.

Note: VAT = value-added tax.

*Significant at the 10 percent level.

[1]Large adjustment episodes in which the primary balance continually improved with no reversal in the first three post-adjustment years, or where reversal was limited, on average to 20 percent of the total adjustment.

Duration Analysis of Large Fiscal Adjustments

A formal duration model was developed to identify the influence of a range of factors on the probability of a successful large fiscal adjustment.[9] The duration analysis technique estimates a hazard function, which is defined as the probability that a fiscal adjustment will be terminated in a particular year, conditional on having had an adjustment in the previous year. To facilitate the interpretation of results, the model estimates the probability of terminating the adjustment only after the thresholds for the "large" adjustment have been reached.[10] The hazard function was estimated through both semiparametric techniques, which do not require an assumption about the func-

---

[9]Previous applications of duration analysis techniques to fiscal adjustment episodes include Gupta and others (2005), which considered emerging markets; Gupta and others (2004), which assessed low-income countries; Adam and Bevan (2004), which covered a cross-section of 127 countries; and Von Hagen, Hallet, and Strauch (2001), which reviewed the adjustment experience of EU countries.

[10]This distinguishes the model from earlier studies. The specification combines advantages of probit estimates of the probability of sustaining the adjustment after a certain period (a clear definition of the initial adjustment period) with advantages of the duration model (an efficient use of all information in the data). The specification also reduces the problem of sample selectivity bias in modeling large adjustments: instead of choosing observations in the sample based on certain characteristics correlated with the endogenous variable, the choice is based on initial conditions.

Table 4.5. Components of Forced Versus Discretionary Fiscal Adjustments
(In percent of the contribution to change in primary balance)

		Of Which:	
	Large Adjustments	Forced	Discretionary
Number of episodes	155	20	21
"Small" reversal rate[1]	42.6	52.4	28.6
"Medium" reversal rate[1]	26.5	15.0	42.9
"Large" reversal rate[1]	16.1	15.0	14.3
Success rate in terms of achieving a sustainable primary balance by end of adjustment episode	72.7	30.0	95.2
Success rate in terms of achieving a sustainable primary balance during the three years after adjustment	51.3	29.4	83.3
Average size of adjustment	12.7	19.5	9.2
Average duration (in years)	2.8	2.4	2.4
Average proportion of adjustment in first year	55.0	64.8	66.3
Primary balance	100.0	100.0	100.0
Total revenues and grants	30.0	11.9**	48.7
Tax revenues, *of which:*	17.3	−0.4**	27.6
Taxes on income, profits, and capital gains, *of which:*	6.9	0.1*	14.4
Individual	1.9	−2.0	4.9
Corporate	4.1	1.0	9.5
Taxes on payroll	0.3	−0.3	0.1
Taxes on property	0.2	0.5	0.9
Domestic taxes on goods and services, *of which:*	5.9	1.1	5.3
General taxes, turnover, VAT	5.1	1.1	4.2
Excises	1.2	1.4	−1.2
Taxes on international trade and transactions, *of which:*	0.4	−0.7	5.1
Import duties	0.9	−0.7	3.8
Export duties	2.1	0.5	1.1
Other taxes	0.4	0.2	0.6
Nontax revenues	7.9	9.0	10.1
Capital revenues	0.6	1.0	1.6
Grants	4.8	3.2	11.0
Unclassified revenues	1.1	0.3	0.2
Total primary expenditure	70.0	88.1*	51.3
Primary current expenditure, *of which:*	31.0	44.3	32.4
Subsidies	14.9	20.8	19.4
Goods and services (excluding wages)	8.9	14.7	5.5
Wages	7.6	8.4	7.4
Unclassified current expenditure	−0.5	0.4	0.1
Capital	25.0	18.5	19.3
Net lending	13.9	25.3**	−0.4
Unclassified expenditure	3.7	12.1	0.5

Sources: IMF, *Government Finance Statistics* (various issues); and IMF staff estimates.

Note: VAT = value-added tax.

* Significant at the 5 percent level.

** Significant at the 1 percent level.

[1]"Small" reversal rates refer to cases in which reversal of adjustment during the first three post-adjustment years is less than 20 percent. "Medium" reversal rates refer to cases in which average reversal of adjustment during the first three post-adjustment years is more than 20 percent but less than 60 percent. "Large" reversal rates refer to cases in which reversal during the first three post-adjustment years is greater than 60 percent.

tional form of duration, and parametric techniques, which impose a specific functional form. The parametric techniques allow for inferences to be drawn about consolidation fatigue.

In the hazard function specification, the explanatory variables included adjustment design, and macroeconomic, institutional, and political factors:

• Design variables included the ratios of (1) changes in expenditures to changes in primary balance; (2) changes in capital expenditures to changes in expenditures; (3) changes in wages to changes in current expenditures cumulated during the adjustment phase; and (4) changes in nontax revenue to changes in revenue.

Table 4.6. Results from Proportional Hazard Model for Duration of Large Fiscal Adjustments[1]

	Cox Estimation (Semiparametric)						Weibull (Parametric)	
	Hazard ratio	(z-value)	Hazard ratio	(z-value)	Hazard ratio	(z-value)	Hazard ratio	(z-value)
Cumulative change in current expenditures/ cumulative change in primary balance in large adjustment (in percent)	0.998	(−2.0)**	0.998	(−2.2)**	0.997	(−1.9)*	0.997	(−2.3)**
In transition countries			1.003	(1.0)				
In emerging markets			1.000	(0.0)				
In OECD countries			0.999	(−0.1)				
Cumulative change in capital expenditures/ cumulative change in expenditures in large adjustment (in percent)	1.002	(2.6)***	1.002	(2.5)**	1.002	(1.7)*	1.002	(1.7)*
Cumulative change in wages/cumulative change in current expenditures in large adjustment (in percent)	1.000	(0.7)	1.000	(0.7)	1.000	(1.7)*	1.000	(1.1)
Cumulative change in nontax revenue/cumulative change in revenue in large adjustment (in percent)	1.000	(−1.5)	1.000	(−1.5)	1.000	(−1.7)*	1.000	(−1.2)
Share of adjustment in the first year (in percent)	1.012	(4.6)***	1.012	(4.5)***	1.009	(3.2)***	1.018	(4.8)***
Inflation (in percent)	0.987	(−3.2)***	0.988	(−3.1)***	0.987	(−2.5)**	0.987	(−2.7)***
U.S. treasury bill interest rate (in percent)	1.056	(1.9)*	1.058	(1.9)*	0.952	(−0.6)	1.112	(3.3)***
Cyclical position (in percent)[2]	1.009	(0.9)	1.010	(1.0)	1.018	(1.5)	1.013	(1.0)
Cumulative change in real exchange rate in large adjustment (in percent)[3]	1.275	(2.9)***	1.237	(2.4)**	1.206	(2.1)**	1.257	(2.0)**
Change in oil prices (in percent)	0.995	(−1.4)	0.995	(−1.4)	0.998	(−0.5)	0.993	(−2.1)**
GDP per capita (1987 PPP prices)	1.000	(−1.4)	1.000	(−1.1)			1.000	(−0.9)
Urban population (in percent)	1.007	(1.6)	1.007	(1.5)			1.012	(2.0)**
Corruption index					0.925	(−1.0)		
Political risk index					0.640	(−1.8)*		
IMF program dummy	0.792	(−1.2)	0.775	(−1.3)	0.725	(−1.3)	0.807	(−1.0)
Weibull shape parameter[4]							0.566	(9.5)***
Number of subjects	113		113		79		113	
Number of failures	96		96		64		96	
Time at risk	291		291		212		291	
Log likelihood	−366.76		−366.54		−218.93		−97.27	
Wald chi-square	57.26		60.09		41.66		78.11	
P-value	0.00		0.00		0.00		0.00	

Sources: IMF staff calculations.
Note: PPP = purchasing power parity.
* Significant at 10 percent level.
** Significant at 5 percent level.
*** Significant at 1 percent level.
[1]A coefficient greater than one implies a positive association of the variable with the probability of ending a large fiscal adjustment.
[2]Residuals from the regression of real GDP on trend.
[3]Bilateral to U.S. dollar.
[4]Values greater than zero denote positive duration dependence.

• Macroeconomic factors included inflation, the U.S. treasury bill rate (a proxy for the world interest rate), the cyclical position at the end of the large adjustment period, cumulative real exchange rate appreciation before reaching the large threshold, and changes in oil prices.

• Institutional characteristics included the level of institutional development, as proxied by GDP per

capita in constant purchasing power parity (PPP) prices, and the share of urban population. In an alternative specification, an index of corruption and a country risk index replaced the last two variables to proxy for institutional characteristics.[11]

[11]Indexes of corruption and political risk come from the *International Country Risk Guide*. See Appendix IV for a more detailed discussion of this technique.

Box 4.2. Political Support for Fiscal Adjustment

The initiation of fiscal adjustment was connected with significant political developments in most of the case study countries. In Canada and New Zealand, majority governments were elected with the mandate to tackle long-standing fiscal issues. The initiation of adjustment in Lithuania came after two governments fell as conditions worsened in 1999 and with a view to establishing policy credibility prior to elections just 10 months later. In Côte d'Ivoire and Zambia, fiscal policy changes were connected with major political developments, including the death of the Ivoirian president in 1993 and Zambia's first multiparty elections after nearly three decades of independence. In Lebanon, fiscal adjustment was viewed as a condition for sustaining post-civil-war reconstruction. The 1998 financial crisis in Russia altered political dynamics and allowed for strengthened taxation of oil companies and improved expenditure control at the local and regional levels, long-standing areas of weakness.

Sustained adjustment took place under broad consensus governments in several of the case study countries. The first democratic elections in post-apartheid South Africa produced a strong majority for the African National Congress, which established credi-

bility by setting and meeting fiscal adjustment targets. The establishment of majority governments also supported sustained consolidation in Finland. Jamaica's People's National Party won strong majorities in 1993, 1997, and 2001, but complex relations with civil service unions and the need to maintain very large primary surpluses to address a substantial debt burden complicated adjustment efforts. In Russia (1993–96), electoral pressures undermined consolidation, and in Lebanon, adjustment was complicated by electoral cycles, complex political arrangements, and lack of political cohesion.

The presence of an external political or economic anchor helped influence adjustment policies, and possibly enhanced "ownership" of consolidation efforts, in some countries. These included a desire to support trade and economic integration arrangements. For Lithuania, the fiscal adjustment was motivated in part by a need to demonstrate effective policy management in line with EU accession. In Finland, adjustment was linked to EMU accession. In Canada, the need to strengthen competitiveness in light of the North American Free Trade Agreement (NAFTA) provided an impetus for adjustment and structural fiscal reforms.

With the exception of the risk index, the coverage of variables was broadly similar to that of earlier studies. The data set covers the 155 large adjustment episodes identified earlier in the paper.

The hazard model defines the end of the adjustment episode by considering the change in the ratio of public debt to GDP, reflecting the debt sustainability analysis applied by the IMF in its surveillance work. Exit occurs when either the primary balance deteriorates or the debt ratio starts to increase after the large primary adjustment had been achieved. This is similar to earlier research, which defined success as a continuous adjustment of the primary balance (a "gradient" approach) or, alternatively, as maintaining a primary balance continuously below a defined threshold (a "level" approach).

The results highlight the importance of fiscal design—the relative contribution of revenue and expenditure measures—in sustaining large adjustments, and they signal an important role for macroeconomic and political factors (Table 4.6).[12] In

particular, the probability of sustaining the adjustment increases with expenditure restraint, particularly if it comes from current expenditures. An adjustment fully based on expenditure reduction is associated with a 30 percent higher probability of success than a revenue-based adjustment.[13] If, in addition, the expenditure adjustment is fully based on current expenditures, the probability of success increases by 20 percent. Reducing wages is correlated with success of the adjustment, although the result is not robust to changes in specification. The proportion of nontax revenues in the revenue effort seems to be associated with a higher probability of success, although the coefficient is not precisely estimated. This may reflect the availability of nondistortionary sources of revenues, such as rents from natural resources.

Conducting an adjustment during a crisis is associated with a higher probability of reversal. The large share of adjustment in the first year, which may indicate a crisis situation, is associated with a higher probability of failure.

---

[12]Some earlier studies used a combination of the two (a "hybrid" approach). The approach applied here might be considered a "hybrid-debt" approach. Tests did not reveal problems with model specification. However, as several explanatory variables proxy—often imprecisely—for unobservable factors and many are insignificant, the fit of the model is not particularly good. Results from alternative specifications (including changes in the definition

of large adjustment) are similar. Also, allowing for unobservable individual random effects to enter the hazard function ("frailty model") does not substantially change the results.

[13]Interacting the share of expenditures in the adjustment with group dummies for transition, emerging market, and OECD countries does not indicate that this effect varies across the groups.

Box 4.3. IMF's Role in Supporting Adjustment Efforts

The case studies suggest that the IMF played a key role in helping member countries diagnose underlying fiscal problems, assess the need for structural fiscal reforms, and design a robust policy response. In some countries, the IMF provided financial support to macroeconomic reform programs (see Appendix Table A3.6). In Russia, for example, the first round of fiscal consolidation was supported by a Stand-By Arrangement in 1995 and an Extended Fund Facility (EFF) arrangement from 1996. The second attempt at fiscal adjustment in Russia was supported by another Stand-By Arrangement in 1999. In Lithuania, fiscal adjustment was the centerpiece of economic reform programs in 2000–02 that were supported by two successive precautionary Stand-By Arrangements. An arrangement under the IMF's Compensatory Financing Facility (CFF) helped the authorities in South Africa mitigate the impact of a drought and low commodity prices in 1993. Adjustment efforts in Côte d'Ivoire were supported by two programs under the Enhanced Structural Adjustment Facility, as well as an arrangement under the Poverty Reduction and Growth Facility (PRGF). A Stand-By Arrangement was agreed upon with Nigeria at the end of the period of fiscal consolidation under review, and adjustment policies in Jamaica were formally monitored by the IMF staff in 2000–02.

The IMF also provided technical assistance (TA) in the design and implementation of structural fiscal reforms in several of the countries. TA was provided in a wide range of areas in Russia (tax policy, tax administration, tax compliance and audit, social safety nets, budgeting and accounting, and treasury operations), Zambia (tax policy, fiscal management, and public expenditure management), and Lithuania (expenditure policy, tax reform, and treasury operations). The IMF's TA also helped country authorities meet fiscal adjustment targets in South Africa (customs administration, capital gains taxation), Lebanon (income and indirect taxes, customs tariffs, and excises), Nigeria (budgeting, VAT), and Côte d'Ivoire (tax administration, budgeting).

Higher domestic inflation, lower world interest rates, and a real exchange rate depreciation facilitate the adjustment. Inflation reduces the domestic debt burden. The result may also reflect the possibility that real spending cuts are easier to undertake politically when there are nominal increases. Lower world interest rates reduce the external debt burden. Depreciation may boost economic activity and revenues in foreign currency, facilitating the adjustment, though depreciation would also increase the domestic counterpart needs of external debt and interest payments. The cyclical positions of and the remaining gap between the primary balance and the debt-stabilizing primary balance are not significant.

Political instability and the quality of institutions are, respectively, negatively and positively associated with the duration of adjustment.[14] Proxies for political instability likely reflect increased fiscal pressures at the time of political tensions and higher debt-service costs due to higher risk premiums. Better institutions maybe related to fiscal policy factors connected with higher levels of development, such as a larger taxable base. Box 4.2 provides a description of political factors in the case study countries.

While the sign of the relevant coefficient suggests that IMF programs are associated with a higher probability of success, the coefficient is not statistically significant. One should not be led to infer that the IMF has played a limited role in fiscal adjustment; in fact, as discussed in Box 4.3, the IMF has played a key role in several of the case study countries.

Results from the parametric model point to the presence of "consolidation fatigue," given that the probability of terminating an adjustment increases with time.

---

[14]While the proxy for political instability is significant in the models, that for the quality of institutions is not significant (at the 10 percent level) for this specification. The share of urban population and GDP per capita are weaker proxies, but are available for a larger group of countries.

V   Macroeconomic Impact of Large Fiscal Adjustments

The economic literature has emphasized that fiscal adjustments may contribute to a range of macroeconomic outcomes, depending on the relative impact of such factors as the direct impact of reduced aggregate demand, eased inflationary pressures and a more competitive real exchange rate, higher national savings and lower interest rates, confidence and wealth effects, and labor market effects.

- The direct impact of lower government expenditures or higher taxes is to reduce aggregate demand. Reduced capital spending may also weaken growth prospects, while lower nonwage expenditures may lower spending efficiency.

- Fiscal adjustment may, however, ease inflationary pressures and promote a more competitive real exchange rate. Consolidation may also promote a more viable external current account and a more sustainable debt burden, lowering the risk premium. A combination of higher national savings, lower interest rates, and a more depreciated currency may lead to higher private investment and net exports.

- High quality fiscal consolidation may help improve the effectiveness of revenues and expenditures, with fewer tax distortions, better expenditure targeting, and enhanced project selection. In turn, economic agents may perceive that their permanent income has risen, or that the returns to investment have increased, thus enhancing consumption and investment.

In cases of particularly large fiscal adjustments, or when initial economic conditions are exceptionally difficult, positive macroeconomic effects may dominate. Giavazzi and Pagano (1990) reviewed the Danish and Irish adjustment episodes of the 1980s and concluded that they were sufficiently large and persistent to alter expectations about future taxation, contributing to a consumption and investment boom. They suggested that smaller consolidations may simply have had conventional, contractionary effects. Subsequent studies have found that spending cuts may be associated with increased private consumption and output growth in countries with high levels of public debt, but may have negative effects when debt levels are low. Expenditure rationalization has been found to contribute to increased national savings in both small and large adjustments, but with stronger effects in cases of large consolidation.[15]

This study uses event studies to reveal a range of stylized facts about macroeconomic developments in the aftermath of large fiscal adjustments. The event studies compare the behavior of a range of key variables before, during, and after large fiscal adjustments. In order to allow for cross-country comparison, all of the variables are standardized by presenting the data in country-specific standard deviations from mean values.[16] Confidence intervals provide a measure of the statistical significance of differences in the macroeconomic variables between nonadjustment and post-adjustment periods, at the 95 percent confidence level.

Overall, the event studies indicate that positive macroeconomic developments tend to accompany large fiscal adjustments. GDP growth recovers sharply to trend during the first two years of the adjustment (Figure 5.1), driven by an improvement in private investment and gradual gains in consumption and the trade balance (Figure A5.1). The trade balance may be responding to a depreciation in the real effective exchange rate, while other components of private demand likely benefit from a reduction in domestic financing to the budget and lower interest rates. Inflation persists above trend two years into the large fiscal adjustment, but then declines. In the sample of small adjustments, a markedly different picture emerges with adjustment accompanied by a mild dampening of growth and inflation, along with a deterioration in the components of private demand. The overall picture suggests that expansionary fiscal con-

---

[15]Perotti (1999); Giavazzi, Jappelli, and Pagano (2000).

[16]The simple, graphical format of the event studies does not impose any parametric structure on the data, and the technique is, by nature, univariate. See Hemming, Kell, and Schimmelpfennig (2003) for a more detailed description of this methodology.

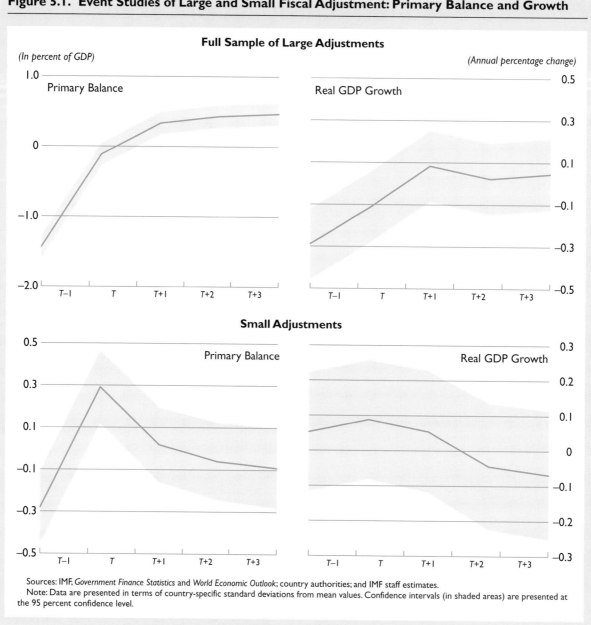

Figure 5.1. Event Studies of Large and Small Fiscal Adjustment: Primary Balance and Growth

Sources: IMF, *Government Finance Statistics* and *World Economic Outlook*; country authorities; and IMF staff estimates.
Note: Data are presented in terms of country-specific standard deviations from mean values. Confidence intervals (in shaded areas) are presented at the 95 percent confidence level.

solidations may be more widespread in developing countries, which form the bulk of the sample, than was previously thought to be the case.

Among large adjustments, the best macroeconomic performance is associated with gradual, sustained consolidations. For *gradual* adjustments (Figure 5.2), there appears to be a stronger upward momentum to GDP growth. These gains appear to come at the expense of a greater degree of inflationary pressure, although consumption remains below

trend (Figure A5.2). While spread-out adjustments are accompanied by more lasting real effective exchange rate depreciations, there appears to be only a relatively modest impact on the trade balance (Figure A5.3). *Sustained* adjustments also show a stronger upward momentum to GDP growth, which seems to be driven by recovery of consumption from a lower base, and greater upward momentum in the trade balance. However, these positive developments again seem to come at the expense of higher infla-

Figure 5.2. Event Studies of Various Types of Large Fiscal Adjustment: Primary Balance and Growth

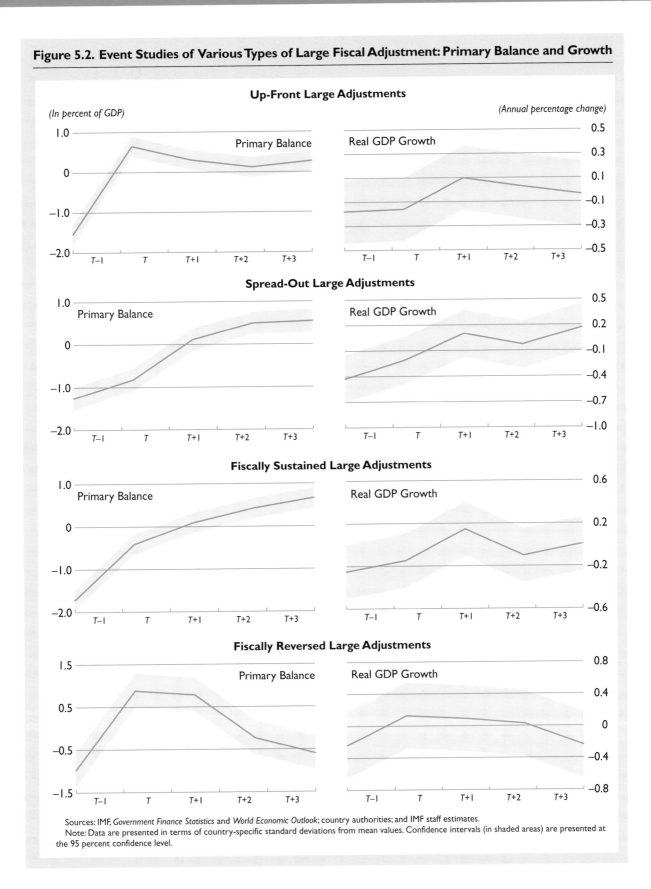

Sources: IMF, *Government Finance Statistics* and *World Economic Outlook*; country authorities; and IMF staff estimates.

Note: Data are presented in terms of country-specific standard deviations from mean values. Confidence intervals (in shaded areas) are presented at the 95 percent confidence level.

tion. The better macroperformance accompanying sustained adjustments is again consistent with an expansionary fiscal contraction.

Among the case studies, economic recovery and improved performance typically followed an initial slowdown and higher unemployment.[17] Recovery tended to be based on lower inflation, strengthened competitiveness, an improved external position, and accelerated growth of private investment. In Lithuania, for example, the unemployment rate initially doubled, but fiscal adjustment helped to sharply reduce the external current account deficit and restore confidence in the country's currency board arrangement. In Zambia, lower domestic financing of the government and improved monetary control contributed to significantly lower inflation and a strengthening of the current account. In New Zealand, consolidation, combined with monetary stabilization, helped reduce inflation and the current account deficit. After a period of output stagnation during 1988–92, growth picked up to an average of 3.5 percent per year during 1993–2001. In Canada, the adjustment also appeared to contribute to an initial slowdown. Thereafter, private investment responded positively, and high growth rates and low inflation were sustained.

---

[17]See Appendix Table A3.5.

Improved economic performance in some countries partly reflected cyclical and commodity price developments, which in turn helped sustain the fiscal adjustment. In Finland, for example, output declined in 1992–93, reflecting a collapse of the financial sector and a consequent fall in domestic demand. This was worsened by the loss of trade with the Baltic countries, Russia, and other countries of the former Soviet Union. Fiscal adjustment contributed to lower inflation and a stronger external position. The emergence of the high-tech sector and an explosion of exports boosted fiscal revenues in the mid- and late 1990s. Lithuania's adjustment was aided by recovery in Russia in the wake of the 1998 financial crisis, although the rebound of growth was driven initially by redirection of exports to western Europe. Higher oil prices helped to sustain the second adjustment effort in Russia, together with improved tax arrangements for the energy sector. In Zambia, renewed grants from donors contributed to an initial improvement in the fiscal balance.

In other countries, complex macroeconomic situations were not positively affected by fiscal adjustment. In Jamaica, high real interest rates and a high tax burden limited growth and may have contributed to a growing informal sector. In Lebanon, high public debt and interest payments contributed to high real interest rates and low growth. These factors were compounded by internal and regional political tensions.

VI Conclusions

The findings of this paper provide a number of suggestions for policymakers on the design and implementation of a large fiscal adjustment. Expenditure measures appear to offer the greatest likelihood of success, in terms of durability of adjustment and favorable macroeconomic impact. To ensure sustainability, adjustment policies will need to take into account the effect of containment of the wage bill and public employment reduction on the quality of services in areas such as health and education. Experience has shown that these considerations are best cast in the context of a multiyear framework.

Fiscal adjustment based on revenue enhancements also offers prospects for durability and greater efficiency, particularly in countries with low initial revenue-to-GDP ratios. Revenue measures need to be broad based and complemented by improvements in tax administration. When countries are confronted with solvency and liquidity crises, however, expenditure-based adjustments appear to be the dominant strategy, likely reflecting the difficulty of raising revenues in an environment

of sharp declines in private economic activity. Under such circumstances, policymakers may not be in a position to select an optimal trade-off between quality and speed of adjustment.

Institutional considerations are important to the design and implementation of fiscal adjustments, with improvements in fiscal institutions providing important support to sustained consolidation. The IMF's technical advice and support for improvements in fiscal transparency helped a large number of the countries covered in the case studies (see Appendix III). A possible extension of this paper would be to consider whether specific institutional arrangements, such as fiscal responsibility laws, have had a significant, measurable impact on the durability of large adjustments.

Finally, the case studies and duration analysis point to the importance of political support for fiscal adjustment. Adjustment design that reflects a clear prioritization of policy objectives through medium-term planning, as well as the protection of important social outlays, will help build and sustain political support.

Appendix I   Data and Definitions

An adjustment episode is defined as any year or succession of years of uninterrupted improvement in the fiscal primary balance, and focuses on the consolidated central government (on a cash basis). In setting this definition, a number of considerations are taken into account:

- The *primary balance* is a more appropriate indicator of the fiscal stance, given the volatility of interest and exchange rates. Indeed, during adjustments accompanied by disinflation, excluding interest is vital to avoid mismeasurement of fiscal effort: in these circumstances, the interest bill can include a large debt amortization component.

- The focus on *uninterrupted improvement* avoids double counting. Earlier studies that were based on a predetermined duration for an adjustment episode often considered contiguous episodes as separate consolidations, potentially biasing results.

- *Noncyclically adjusted data* were used due to data limitations. Cyclical adjustment may not be of critical importance in this type of analysis. For example, Adam and Bevan (2004) found no relation between lagged GDP and the fiscal balance in their sample of 127 countries.

- *Data for the consolidated central government on a cash basis* were used also due to data limitations. Using data on a commitment basis or using a general government or even broader public sector concept (and including contingent liabilities such as pension entitlements) would have better reflected the underlying fiscal stance, but such data were not available for the full sample of countries.

- *Data on fiscal outcomes* were used, again due to data limitations. To limit cases of unintended adjustment, episodes for oil exporters were excluded for periods of significant increases in real oil prices.[18] Cases of targeted "large" adjustments that do not reach the threshold would also present significant conceptual problems, because targets can change over the course of an adjustment.

---

[18]Specifically, for countries with oil exports in excess of 25 percent of GDP during any five-year period, an episode was excluded if it took place during 1973, 1979–80, 1999–2000, when real oil prices increased by over 10 percent. This eliminated 35 episodes, including 20 that would be considered large. Use of the nonresource primary balance would best address the exogeneity problem. The data necessary to construct these balances are not readily available, however.

Table A1.1. Data Set: Country Coverage[1]

Developed Countries (24)	Emerging Markets (22)	Transition Economies (24)	Developing Economies (95)		
Australia	Argentina	Albania	Algeria	Ecuador	Libya	Samoa
Austria	Brazil	Armenia	Antigua and Barbuda	El Salvador	Madagascar	São Tomé and Príncipe
Belgium	Chile	Azerbaijan	Bahamas, The	Equatorial Guinea	Malawi	Saudi Arabia
Canada	Colombia	Belarus	Bahrain	Eritrea	Maldives	Senegal
Denmark	Cyprus	Bulgaria	Bangladesh	Ethiopia	Mali	Seychelles
Finland	Egypt	Croatia	Barbados	Fiji	Mauritania	Sierra Leone
France	India	Czech Republic	Belize	Gabon	Mauritius	Solomon Islands
Germany	Indonesia	Estonia	Benin	Gambia, The	Morocco	Sri Lanka
Greece	Israel	Georgia	Bhutan	Ghana	Mozambique	Suriname
Iceland	Jordan	Hungary	Bolivia	Grenada	Myanmar	Swaziland
Ireland	Korea, Rep. of	Kazakhstan	Botswana	Guatemala	Namibia	Syrian Arab Republic
Italy	Malaysia	Kyrgyz Republic	Burkina Faso	Guinea	Nepal	Tanzania
Japan	Mexico	Latvia	Burundi	Guinea-Bissau	Netherlands Antilles	Togo
Luxembourg	Pakistan	Lithuania	Cambodia	Guyana	Nicaragua	Tonga
Malta	Peru	Macedonia, FYR	Cameroon	Haiti	Niger	Trinidad and Tobago
Netherlands	Philippines	Moldova	Cape Verde	Honduras	Oman	Tunisia
New Zealand	Singapore	Mongolia	Central African Rep.	Iran, I.R. of	Panama	Uganda
Norway	South Africa	Poland	Chad	Jamaica	Papua New Guinea	Vanuatu
Portugal	Thailand	Romania	Comoros	Kenya	Paraguay	Yemen, Rep. of
Spain	Turkey	Russia	Congo, Rep. of	Kiribati	Qatar	Zambia
Sweden	Uruguay	Slovak Republic	Costa Rica	Kuwait	Rwanda	Zimbabwe
Switzerland	Venezuela	Slovenia	Côte d'Ivoire	Lao P.D.R.	St. Kitts and Nevis	
United Kingdom		Tajikistan	Djibouti	Lebanon	St. Lucia	
United States		Uzbekistan	Dominica	Lesotho	St. Vincent and the	
			Dominican Rep.	Liberia	Grenadines	

Sources: IMF, *Government Finance Statistics* (various issues), *International Financial Statistics* (various issues), *World Economic Outlook*, and *Monitoring of Fund Arrangements*; IMF staff estimates; and country authorities.

[1]Countries excluded due to lack of data are Angola, Brunei Darussalam, China, Democratic Republic of the Congo, Hong Kong SAR, Nigeria, Sudan, Taiwan Province of China, Turkmenistan, and Ukraine.

Table A1.2. Data Sources and Transformations

Variable List	Sources
Fiscal (at the central government level)	For all fiscal and financing data: IMF, *Government Finance Statistics*
Total revenues and grants	(GFS); country authorities; and IMF staff estimates.
Tax revenues, *of which*:	
Taxes on income, profits, and capital gains	
Domestic taxes on goods and services	
Taxes on international trade and transactions	
Nontax revenues	
Capital revenues	
Grants	
Total primary expenditure	
Primary current expenditure, *of which*:	
Subsidies	
Goods and services (excluding wages)	
Wages	
Capital	
Net lending	
Domestic financing	
External financing	
Macroeconomic	IMF, *World Economic Outlook*; and country authorities.
Real GDP growth	IMF, *International Financial Statistics* (IFS), *World Economic Outlook*;
CPI inflation	country authorities; and IMF staff estimates.
Trade balance	IMF, IFS, and *World Economic Outlook*.
Real consumption growth (deflated by CPI)	IMF, IFS; and country authorities.
Real investment growth (deflated by CPI)	IMF, IFS, and *World Economic Outlook*.
Central government debt	IMF, GFS; country authorities; and IMF staff estimates.
Other	
IMF program years by country	IMF, *Monitoring of Fund Arrangements*.

Sources: IMF, *Government Finance Statistics* (various issues), *International Financial Statistics* (various issues), *World Economic Outlook*, and *Monitoring of Fund Arrangements*; IMF staff estimates; and country authorities.

Appendix II   Large Fiscal Adjustment Episodes

Table A2.1. Large Fiscal Adjustment Episodes[1]

Country	Start	Length (years)	Size (GDP)[2]	Size (government)[3]	First Year Adjustment (in percent)[4]
Albania	1997	2	8.0	29.4	26.9
Algeria	1995	2	8.0	26.0	41.5
Antigua and Barbuda	1983	3	8.1	22.4	48.1
Armenia	1995	1	9.1	22.2	100.0
Australia	1994	5	6.3	25.1	8.3
Bahrain	1988	1	13.9	30.8	100.0
Barbados	1992	2	9.2	30.0	82.7
Belize	1987	2	15.2	51.5	30.6
	1994	3	7.2	23.7	24.4
Bhutan	1993	1	8.2	23.8	100.0
Botswana	1973	3	17.9	45.4	47.0
	1982	5	23.4	64.2	2.3
	2000	2	15.4	36.4	83.2
Brazil	1989	2	7.7	30.2	42.9
	1992	3	8.2	44.1	54.9
Bulgaria	1994	1	12.2	34.2	100.0
Burkina Faso	1989	1	8.7	45.3	100.0
Burundi	1997	4	7.8	29.1	29.2
Cameroon	1988	2	9.0	30.2	81.9
	1991	7	9.9	48.9	8.5
Canada	1993	5	6.8	26.5	1.3
Cape Verde	2001	1	15.2	34.1	100.0
Central African Republic	1992	5	11.7	46.1	27.9
Chad	1993	3	9.7	36.6	14.4
Chile	1973	4	8.8	47.0	18.2
Comoros	1985	4	17.4	32.4	19.6
Congo, Republic of	1994	3	15.3	52.3	26.9
Côte d'Ivoire	1994	3	15.1	50.4	36.3
Cyprus	1984	3	6.9	21.8	67.3
Denmark	1983	4	15.5	35.3	14.9
Dominica	1980	1	18.0	36.4	100.0
Ecuador	1984	2	7.1	51.9	42.3
	1988	3	11.0	67.1	37.0
El Salvador	1982	5	7.7	44.4	5.6
Equatorial Guinea	1997	2	17.1	81.3	37.1
Eritrea	1996	2	18.9	26.3	24.9
Fiji	1998	1	11.5	38.9	100.0
Finland	1993	8	24.3	49.4	13.9
Gambia, The	1986	1	10.4	30.0	100.0
	1989	1	13.0	30.5	100.0
Ghana	1977	4	6.9	30.9	22.6
Greece	1978	2	11.9	30.8	96.8
	1990	3	20.3	38.3	9.3
	1998	3	6.9	22.8	14.6
Grenada	1991	3	9.4	25.8	52.1
Guinea	1997	3	6.6	43.0	4.4

Table A2.1 *(continued)*

Country	Start	Length (years)	Size (GDP)[2]	Size (government)[3]	First Year Adjustment (in percent)[4]
Guinea-Bissau	1986	2	26.4	43.4	61.1
	1993	3	22.2	51.1	43.9
	1998	2	9.4	23.0	34.7
Guyana	1974	1	9.2	32.5	100.0
	1977	2	14.1	33.1	85.7
	1987	2	18.1	27.8	46.0
	1990	4	19.0	41.1	24.8
Honduras	1994	2	8.3	35.5	57.4
Hungary	1994	2	10.9	22.2	10.9
Iceland	1978	5	8.6	24.6	21.2
	1995	5	11.3	28.2	3.9
Iran, Islamic Republic of	1981	2	8.0	23.0	43.2
	1989	2	8.3	35.1	70.4
Israel	1982	5	25.6	35.5	25.1
Jamaica	1980	2	10.0	24.3	87.4
	1983	2	12.8	35.8	0.9
	1990	2	7.1	25.0	85.9
	1997	4	13.4	45.6	36.6
Japan	1979	10	6.5	40.4	6.7
Jordan	1979	5	17.9	33.9	77.5
	1988	5	17.3	50.2	11.4
Kenya	1990	3	6.7	26.2	39.8
Kiribati	1997	2	34.7	31.1	96.3
Kuwait	1986	1	24.7	48.2	100.0
	1996	2	18.2	36.9	24.3
Kyrgyz Republic	1996	2	8.6	26.2	92.5
Lebanon	1998	2	10.2	35.7	72.2
Lesotho	1988	3	18.0	34.6	13.1
Liberia	1982	3	8.8	27.8	15.6
Lithuania	1994	5	6.7	22.9	20.6
Malawi	1981	2	9.5	26.3	53.9
	1994	1	6.9	23.2	100.0
	1996	2	12.1	32.9	92.6
Malaysia	1983	3	16.3	42.1	45.3
Maldives	1981	2	14.8	48.8	85.7
	1984	2	8.4	27.6	98.1
	1987	2	9.8	32.2	99.5
Mali	1990	1	6.3	25.1	100.0
Mauritania	1981	7	19.4	63.4	16.9
	1994	3	14.5	44.3	28.5
Mauritius	1982	6	13.4	42.9	15.4
Mexico	1983	1	10.9	42.5	100.0
Moldova	1998	4	8.6	22.3	56.6
Mongolia	1994	2	10.5	23.4	73.6
	1999	3	7.6	22.6	17.5
Morocco	1977	4	8.6	22.2	23.8
Mozambique	1987	3	9.2	30.3	54.3
Myanmar	1974	1	6.6	36.7	100.0
Namibia	1988	2	9.0	22.3	36.5
Nepal	1993	3	7.1	37.6	55.2
New Zealand	1984	5	13.3	29.0	18.2
Nicaragua	1989	1	23.1	46.5	100.0
	1991	1	21.4	47.4	100.0
Oman	1977	1	15.5	24.8	100.0
	1987	1	17.7	36.5	100.0
	1989	2	9.5	23.6	28.9
	1993	5	11.4	30.0	14.0
Panama	1980	1	8.4	27.0	100.0
	1989	4	11.9	46.4	6.2
Papua New Guinea	1994	2	7.1	24.2	48.4
Russia	1995	1	7.2	34.1	100.0

Table A2.1 *(concluded)*

Country	Start	Length (years)	Size (GDP)[2]	Size (government)[3]	First Year Adjustment (in percent)[4]
St. Kitts and Nevis	1988	3	18.9	35.6	58.1
St. Vincent and the Grenadines	1998	4	10.9	26.8	69.4
Samoa	1995	1	27.9	36.3	100.0
São Tomé & Príncipe	1995	3	14.3	22.8	45.7
Saudi Arabia	1988	3	23.1	34.4	30.7
	1992	1	20.9	30.4	100.0
Seychelles	1987	1	19.1	32.6	100.0
	1994	1	29.9	39.0	100.0
	1997	1	18.3	35.8	100.0
Sierra Leone	1987	4	10.9	68.3	10.4
Singapore	1987	4	9.4	27.5	17.3
South Africa	1988	2	7.1	25.4	25.4
	1994	6	8.1	27.9	40.9
Sri Lanka	1983	2	6.5	22.6	58.2
Suriname	1987	4	20.2	40.8	3.6
	1992	3	20.7	48.3	27.1
	2001	1	15.8	39.6	100.0
Swaziland	1974	2	17.3	59.0	52.6
	1979	2	18.1	41.5	70.3
	1987	3	9.2	33.4	67.0
Sweden	1994	5	15.9	33.0	19.6
Tajikistan	1996	4	6.6	27.8	57.6
Tanzania	1983	3	7.9	25.6	71.2
	1987	2	6.5	31.2	95.4
Thailand	1986	5	8.7	48.1	14.2
	2000	2	7.9	30.9	96.5
Togo	1979	2	28.5	49.6	79.2
	1982	2	6.6	22.7	65.1
	1994	4	11.9	52.5	45.4
Tonga	1993	2	10.7	24.5	79.4
Trinidad and Tobago	1987	5	9.2	26.4	14.1
Turkey	1997	2	8.5	35.3	53.9
United Kingdom	1994	5	10.9	25.5	24.0
United States	1993	8	6.5	29.9	8.8
Vanuatu	1987	1	10.9	32.1	100.0
	1999	1	9.5	27.9	100.0
Venezuela, República Bolivariana de	1983	3	9.1	34.6	23.2
	1995	2	6.4	33.1	34.9
Yemen, Republic of	1991	1	8.1	27.0	100.0
	1995	4	12.4	49.5	74.2
Zambia	1974	1	29.1	46.1	100.0
	1983	1	12.8	32.0	100.0
	1987	1	8.5	24.2	100.0
	1990	3	12.8	47.7	12.2
	1994	2	7.7	30.3	92.2
Zimbabwe	1993	2	7.8	25.3	65.1

Sources: IMF, *Government Finance Statistics* (various issues); and IMF staff estimates.

[1]An episode of fiscal adjustment is defined as a period of continuous improvement of the primary balance of the consolidated central government that exceeds 6.3 percent of GDP and 21.8 percent of initial consolidated central government expenditures in the year prior to commencement.

[2]Total consolidation of central government primary balance during the adjustment episode.

[3]Total adjustment in percent of consolidated central government expenditures in the year prior to commencement of the episode.

[4]Extent of consolidation in the first year, as a share of the total adjustment during the episode.

Appendix III   Case Studies of Large Fiscal Adjustment

Thirteen case studies were prepared to supplement the empirical analysis.[19] The case studies offer further evidence about success and adjustment design and allow examination of specific measures and supporting institutional, macroeconomic, and political factors.[20] Half of the adjustments covered by the case studies were expenditure based and half were revenue based. Likely reflecting borrowing constraints, consolidation was intended to be front-loaded in 8 of the 12 cases, involving an adjustment of 5 percentage points of GDP or more over just one or two years.

The findings of the case studies are summarized in Tables A3.1–A3.6.

---

[19]Case studies were prepared by Thomas Baunsgaard, Ana Corbacho, Stephan Danninger, Lubin Doe, Stefano Fassina, Mark Flanagan, Mark Horton, and Antonio Spilimbergo. Other examples of fiscal adjustment in developing and emerging market countries have been assessed in recent papers by the IMF staff and the Independent Evaluation Office (IEO), including, Hemming, Kell, and Schimmelpfennig (2003), which covered 11 cases of fiscal vulnerability and financial crisis; IEO (2003b), which reviewed developments in Brazil, Indonesia, and Korea; IEO (2004), which reviewed fiscal adjustment in Argentina; and IEO (2003a), which reviewed fiscal adjustment in 15 country cases.

---

[20]Three of the case studies are not among the 155 large adjustment episodes identified from the data set: the second consolidation effort in Russia and the adjustment in Lithuania, both of which extend in time beyond 2001, the end of the period covered by the data set, and the consolidation in Nigeria, for which there were gaps in the annual data. These three cases were selected to provide insight into adjustment in transition countries, into complex fiscal federalism aspects, and into oil issues.

Table A3.1. Context for Adjustment

Episode	Political Background	Macroeconomic Background	Government Finances	Structural Reform Issues
Brazil 1999–2003	Social Democratic Party (PSDB) reelected in 1999. The left-wing Workers' Party (PT) elected in 2003. Increased consensus on the need for fiscal austerity.	External and fiscal crisis, stemming from contagion from Asia, rising current account deficit, and loose fiscal policy; sharp exchange rate devaluation in early 1999 and adoption of a flexible exchange rate; low growth and inflation.	Increasing primary fiscal deficits at all levels of government and a rise in public debt. High tax burden; large social security imbalances; need for sub-national fiscal discipline; loss-making public enterprises.	Labor market rigidities; financial sector problems; fairly restricted trade system; cumbersome tax system; generous pensions; significant budget rigidities.
Canada 1993–2000	Majority federal government elected in 1993 to address fiscal issues; similar election results in 1994–95 in the two largest provinces.	Recovery from recession; low inflation; high output gap and unemployment; exchange rate depreciation; improving current account balance.	Sizable deficit and debt stock; large share of debt held at short term and by nonresidents; high tax ratio; expanding entitlements; sub-federal fiscal issues.	Labor market rigidities; interprovincial trade barriers.
Côte d'Ivoire 1993–2000	Period of political instability following the death in 1993 of president who had governed for 33 years.	Growth stagnated during 1987–93, with declines in 1992–93, partly due to strong currency; high and increasing public debt (over 170 percent of GDP in 1993); low inflation.	High deficit (12 percent of GDP in 1992–93); tax revenues declined from 20–22 percent of GDP in late 1980s to less than 15 percent; high wage (11 percent of GDP) and interest (9½ percent) bills.	High trade taxes (maximum import tariff of nearly 200 percent); CFA franc devalued by 50 percent in January 1994.

Table A3.1 *(continued)*

Episode	Political Background	Macroeconomic Background	Government Finances	Structural Reform Issues
Finland 1992–2000	Coalition elected in 1991; grand coalition from 1995, with mandate for EMU membership.	Deep recession; high output gap; rising unemployment; low inflation; exchange rate depreciation; improving current account.	High deficit and rapidly increasing debt ratio; high tax ratio; expanding entitlement programs.	Banking sector crisis; labor market rigidities; response to collapse of the Soviet Union.
Jamaica 1998–2001	Four successive electoral victories for People's National Party (PNP) from 1989, including strong majority victory in late 1997. Close ties of PNP and main opposition party to public service unions.	High inflation and stagnant output in the early 1990s. From 1996, exchange stability and lower inflation, but with high interest rates, real appreciation, declining output, and high current account deficit. 1996–97 financial crisis.	Fiscal balance worsened by 8 percent of GDP in 1996–97, partly reflecting support for troubled financial institutions. High interest bill; wage bill pressures.	Large and growing informal sector; financial sector problems; high crime rates; vulnerability to tourism receipts and swings in bauxite prices.
Lebanon 1998–2002	1989 accord ended long civil war. Earlier adjustment undermined by weak support, high oil prices, and civil conflict in south. From 1998, new government-supported adjustment.	Debt grew from 30 percent of GDP in 1992 to over 100 percent in 1997. Moderate growth in mid-1990s; inflation reduced. Real exchange rate appreciation and lack of structural reforms affected competitiveness and export growth.	Narrow tax base (15 percent of GDP) and high spending on rebuilding (9 percent of GDP per year during 1995–97); high wage bill (11 percent of GDP) and debt service. Deficit was 27 percent in 1997, with primary deficit of 12 percent of GDP.	Continuing reconstruction; conflict in south Lebanon; inefficient public services (electricity, ports).
Lithuania 1999–2003	Succession of prime ministers in the run-up to initiation of adjustment. New government faced deepening fiscal crisis with elections within one year.	Deep recession following 1998 financial crisis in Russia; growing unemployment; high current account deficit; low inflation, with currency peg to U.S. dollar.	Deficit worsened in 1998–99, reflecting recession, increased household transfers, and lending to state oil company. Poor expenditure management and large stock of payment arrears; moderate tax and debt burdens.	Labor market rigidities; energy tariffs below cost recovery; trade restrictions and agriculture subsidies; EU accession-related reforms.
New Zealand 1983–88	Majority government elected in 1984 with mandate to address fiscal and structural issues.	Recovery from recession, low unemployment, moderate inflation (price controls), increasing current account deficit, exchange rate depreciation.	High deficit and debt ratio, much of debt foreign-held; narrow tax base; expanding entitlement programs.	Heavily regulated product markets; rigid labor markets; inefficient state sector; recently abandoned financial market controls.
Nigeria 1990–2000	Military regimes in place prior to 1999 democratic transition. Numerous allegations of corruption, fraud, and theft during Abacha regime (1993–98).	GDP growth slowed from nearly 9 percent per year in 1988–90 to 1.9 percent in 1993 and 0.3 percent in 1994. Inflation increased over the same period, exceeding 70 percent in 1994.	Overall balance weakened from surplus of 2.9 percent of GDP in 1992 to 11.2 percent deficit in 1993. Non-oil primary deficit in excess of 40 percent of GDP. Modest non-oil revenues (5 percent of GDP) and fluctuating expenditures.	Dual-exchange rate system; large informal sector; corruption and governance concerns; oil dependency; subsidies (fertilizer).
Russia 1995–98	Violent October 1993 political confrontation; Duma elections in 1994 and 1995; key presidential elections in 1996.	Severe economic contraction and hyperinflation during 1992–94, with inflation over 300 percent in 1994 and output decline of 13½ percent.	Deficit increased from 6½ percent of GDP in 1993 to 11½ percent in 1994, due to growth of subsidies to industry and agriculture.	Profound post-Soviet structural transformation began with price reform in 1992 and privatization during 1992–94.

Table A3.1 *(concluded)*

Episode	Political Background	Macroeconomic Background	Government Finances	Structural Reform Issues
Russia 1999–2002	1998 financial crisis changed dynamics, with improved taxation of energy and spending control at sub-national levels. Succession of prime ministers and resignation of president in 1999.	Debt default in August 1998 and depreciation of the ruble. GDP decline of 4.9 percent in 1998, with pick-up of inflation from 15 percent in 1997 to 28 percent in 1998 and 85 percent in 1999.	Central government tax revenues declined through mid-1990s, reaching 9 percent of GDP in 1998 due in part to depressed oil prices. High tax arrears, mutual offsets, and barter payments.	Continuing transition, with major distortions in the business environment and the energy sector; large informal economy.
South Africa 1993–2001	Transition to majority rule and government of national unity in April 1994. Consensus policy bodies established before and after transition.	Recession in 1990–92, with higher inflation, capital flight, and concerns with transition. Apartheid-era trade and financial sanctions lifted in October 1993.	Deficit worsened during 1990–93 by 5 percentage points, due to revenue weakness, social spending, and drought relief. Increasing public debt, although moderate at 40 percent of GDP. Low external debt.	Apartheid-era distortions in labor markets, trade, public enterprises, and public administration. Wide disparities in income, wealth, and skills.
Zambia 1989–94	First multiparty elections in October 1991.	High inflation; external arrears.	Deficit averaged over 11 percent of GDP during 1987–89, due to poor revenues and increasing expenditures (maize and fertilizer subsidies).	Controls on prices, exchange rate, and international transactions; agriculture subsidies; large informal sector.

Sources: Country authorities; and IMF staff reports.

Table A3.2. Adjustment Design

Episode	Adjustment Basis	Size and Timing	Revenue Measures	Expenditure Measures
Brazil 1999–2003	Revenues	Targeted 3 percent of GDP increase in the primary surplus in 1999. Gradual increase in the target to 4.25 percent of GDP in 2003.	Nonfinancial public sector revenues increased by 8 percent of GDP during 1999–2003. Improvements in revenue administration. Privatization and increased commercial orientation of public enterprises.	Nonfinancial public sector total expenditures also increased by 7 percent of GDP during 1999–2003, despite measures to contain nonentitlement spending. To ensure compliance with primary surplus targets, expenditure was curtailed particularly during the first part of the year, until revenue performance was certified. Strengthening of social safety nets. Pension reform to reduce generous benefits.
Canada 1993–2000	Expenditures	3½ percent of GDP reduction in the overall deficit targeted for 1993/94 and 1995/96; provinces targeted 1¾ percent deficit cut.	Amounted to 0.4 percent of GDP through higher excises, broadening of the bases of the personal (PIT) and corporate (CIT) income taxes, and higher CIT rate.	Amounted to 3 percent of GDP, with cuts in defense, wages, employment, unemployment insurance, and agricultural and business subsidies. Cuts in transfers to provinces.
Côte d'Ivoire 1993–2000	Revenues	Primary balance improvement of 5 percent of GDP targeted in 1994, 1.2 percent in 1995, and 0.5 percent in 1996. Second three-year program (1998–2000) targeted 1½ percent of GDP improvement of the primary surplus.	Trade taxes and commodity revenues to increase by 6.1 percent of GDP with devaluation. Maximum tariff cut from 195 to 35 percent; VAT rate cut from 25 to 20 percent. Export taxes on coffee and cocoa reintroduced. In second program, tax exemptions eliminated, minimum 5 percent import tax introduced, and property tax extended.	Compression of civil service real wages, personnel reduction of 1.5 percent. Reorientation of spending to health, education, rural development, and basic infrastructure.
Finland 1992–2000	Expenditures	8 percent reduction in the deficit by 1997 to stabilize debt-to-GDP ratio below 70 percent. Second effort targeted 4.5 percent of GDP reduction in the deficit in 1996, and 1–1.5 percent of GDP reduction in each of two subsequent years.	Broadly revenue-neutral tax reform measures, with increases of user fees in health and education. Second program included broadly revenue-neutral tax reform measures. Higher payroll taxes and employee contributions for social security.	Amounted to 9 percent of GDP in spending cuts planned by the third year, focusing on municipal and social security transfers, capital spending, subsidies, and wages. Second effort targeted 4 percent of GDP in new measures, including subsidies (0.6 percent), social security (0.6), and local transfers (0.8). Some social benefits cut.
Jamaica 1998–2001	Revenues	Targeted improvement in public sector primary balance by 7.8 percent over two years. (1) 2000 Staff Monitored Program (SMP) targeted improvement of central government primary balance by 1.7 percent of GDP for 2000/01 and 2001/02; (2) 2002 SMP targeted 2.4 percent improvement of the central government and public sector primary balances in 2002/03.	Gain of 3.8 percent of GDP targeted through tax administration, higher fuel taxes, and user fees. (1) Decline of 0.3 percent of GDP, due to lower cellular licenses and bauxite revenues; tax gains of 1.1 percent of GDP from VAT extension, elimination of exemptions, and higher interest withholding; (2) gains of 1.6 percent of GDP from VAT extension, exemptions, taxation of derivatives, and compliance.	Cuts in capital expenditure (2.2 percent) and nonwage goods and services (1 percent); moderate wage increase (0.2 percent). Increase of interest bill by 4.1 percent of GDP to 14.3 percent. (1) Targeted cuts in noninterest spending of 2.1 percent of GDP, nonwage goods and services (1.8 percent), and capital (0.2 percent); (2) noninterest cuts of 0.8 percent of GDP, targeting wage bill (0.3 percent), nonwage goods and services (0.3 percent), and capital (0.2 percent).
Lebanon 1998–2002	Expenditures	Targeted 11 percent of GDP reduction of the primary balance in 1998 and 14 percent reduction over five years, with further 0.8 percent of GDP adjustment targeted for 1999 and 3.1 percent for 2000–02.	Targeted 4 percent of GDP increase through higher customs tariffs, new tax on hotel and restaurant services, higher receipts from cellular contracts, and increases in fees and excises (cement, road use, cargo, passport, work permits).	Targeted 7 percent cut in noninterest spending, focused on public investment, transfers, and a wage bill freeze, with cuts in the number of teachers and contractual employees.

Table A3.2 *(concluded)*

Episode	Adjustment Basis	Size and Timing	Revenue Measures	Expenditure Measures
Lithuania 1999–2003	Expenditures	Targeted reduction of the overall deficit by 5.7 percent of GDP in first year and by 2.8 percent of GDP (to a balanced position) in second year.	Amounted to 1.2 percent of GDP in the first year targeted through increased payroll tax and fuel and tobacco excises. Weaker personal income taxes envisaged.	Amounted to 4.5 percent of GDP through cuts in net lending (2.2 percent) and household transfers (2.1 percent); capital spending and wage bill (0.4 percent) through a nominal wage cut.
New Zealand 1983–88	Expenditures	Targeted 7 percent reduction in the overall deficit between 1984/85 and 1986/87. Subsequent effort targeted 3 percent of GDP in measures in 1986/87 to contain deterioration of deficit.	Amounted to 1.5 percent of GDP by third year through PIT base broadening, excise increases, and enterprise dividends. Later effort included 1 percent of GDP through broadening of PIT and CIT bases; excises increased.	Amounted to 2 percent of GDP by third year. Cuts in agricultural and industrial subsidies (including by raising utility prices). Subsequent effort targeted 2 percent of GDP cuts in wages, operations and maintenance, subsidies, and grants.
Nigeria 1990–2000	Revenues	Two adjustment periods: 1995–97 and 1999–2000. During 1999–2000, improved overall balance, but deterioration of the non-oil primary balance.	Introduction of VAT; increased oil prices for domestic consumption (although large subsidy remained). In second period, higher oil prices and elimination of dual exchange rate system from late 1998.	Fertilizer subsidy removed; expenditure compression; reduction of wage bill. Expenditures reduced by overvalued official exchange rate. Higher wages in 2000 to offset compression and increased spending due to reforms of federal structure.
Russia 1995–98	Revenues	Targeted 5½ percent of GDP reduction of the federal deficit in 1995 and further reduction by 2 percent of GDP in 1996.	Increased excises on natural gas and crude oil, increased gasoline taxes, reduction in zero-rated imports, and compliance improvements.	Unspecified, across-the-board real spending cuts of 15 percent.
Russia 1999–2002	Mixed	Targeted adjustment of 2¾ percent of GDP in 1999, half from revenues and half from expenditure cuts.	Strengthening of tax collection from oil companies, helped by the introduction of new oil taxes and high oil prices. Collections centralized at federal level. Cash tax payments required.	No specific areas targeted for real spending cuts. Improved expenditure control by limiting access of some ministries to special funds.
South Africa 1993–2001	Expenditures	Targeted 4 percent of GDP deficit reduction over five years; 2 percent in year one and ½ percent annually thereafter. Subsequent effort announced in 1996 targeted further deficit reduction by 2 percent of GDP from the 1995/96 out-turn.	Revenue neutral from 1994/95, with elimination of exemptions, extension of tax bases, and lower rates. VAT rate increased from 10 to 14 percent in 1993/94. Continued reforms in tax policy and administration.	Targeted cuts in wage bill, subsidies, and transfers and 1 percent of GDP increase of capital expenditures. In second effort, cuts in the wage bill of 3 percent of GDP targeted. Further reorientation of spending on health, education, land reform, and welfare.
Zambia 1989–94	Revenues		Market exchange rate used for import taxation; removal of import tax exemptions; adjustment of PIT brackets, reduction of top marginal rate, extension of PIT to fringe benefits; extension of sales tax; introduction of copper windfall levy; increased fees; mandatory dividends from state-owned enterprises. Sales tax introduced on fuel; improved collection of tax arrears of parastatals.	Reduced maize and fertilizer subsidies and reoriented spending from investment to spending on operations and maintenance and essential goods and services.

Sources: Country authorities; and IMF staff reports.

Table A3.3. Impact of Fiscal Adjustment

Episode	Fiscal Impact	Durability of Fiscal Impact
Brazil 1999–2003	The public sector primary balance improved from a deficit of 1 percent of GDP in 1998 to a surplus of 4.4 percent of GDP in 2003. All levels of government contributed to the turnaround in fiscal outcomes. Fiscal targets on the primary balance were consistently met throughout the period. The overall deficit remained about 4.5 percent of GDP in 1999–2003.	Durable. Fiscal performance has remained strong during 2004, exceeding targets by wide margins. The Budget Guidelines Law maintains the primary surplus target of 4.25 percent of GDP for 2005–07. The overall deficit has fallen sharply since the third quarter of 2003, allowing net public debt to decline to under 57 percent of GDP in October 2004. The composition of federal debt has improved considerably.
Canada 1993–2000	General government primary balance improved by 10 percent of GDP, 7.8 percent due to spending reductions. Targets met for first three years, and exceeded in subsequent two years by over 2 percent, due to conservative budgeting.	Durable. General government maintained a surplus through 2002, 8.5 percentage points above the initial 1993 position, despite a growth slowdown. Debt reduced from 100 percent to 61 percent of GDP.
Côte d'Ivoire 1993–2000	Overall balance improved by 13 percent of GDP from 1993–2001, with reversal in 1999. Strong initial boost in trade taxes (7 percent of GDP), with wage compression and cuts in other current spending. Primary balance improved by 8½ percent of GDP until 1996, before weakening in 1997–99. Primary balance strengthened again during 2000–01. Arrears increased.	Relatively durable. The primary surplus exceeded 2½ percent of GDP in every year but one during 1994–2002. The public debt ratio decreased from nearly 200 percent of GDP in 1994 to just over 100 percent in 1998–2001. Spending was reduced by 12 percentage points of GDP during 1994–2001, reflecting lower interest payments (5 percent of GDP) and a lower wage bill (5 percent). Tax revenues slipped by 3 percentage points of GDP during 1995–97, as trade taxes declined.
Finland 1992–2000	General government primary balance improved by 15.6 percent of GDP, half from revenue, half from expenditure. There were initial shortfalls relative to targets and the deficit rose by 4.5 percent of GDP in 1992 due to recession.	Durable. General government maintained a surplus in 2002 (10 percent above initial 1993 position) despite growth slowdown. Debt has been reduced from 58 to 42 percent of GDP (public accounts basis).
Jamaica 1998–2001	Overall improvement of central government and public sector primary balances by 6.0 percent of GDP, one-third from revenue gains and two-thirds from cuts in noninterest expenditures.	Questionable. Public sector primary surpluses averaged 10½ percent of GDP from 1999/2000 to 2001/02, with little scope for further improvement due to high interest burden (14 percent of GDP) and high wage bill. Weak revenues and increased spending on wages, security, and tourism promotion in 2001/02. Public debt rose to 155 percent of GDP in 2003.
Lebanon 1998–2002	Primary balance improved by 13.9 percent of GDP during 1998–2002, concentrated in 1998–99. Slippage in 2000. Noninterest expenditures cut by 8.1 percent of GDP; revenues increased by 5.7 percent. Expenditure cuts concentrated on capital spending (6.9 percent of GDP) and goods and services (2 percent). Wage bill increased by 0.7 percent of GDP. Revenues boosted by introduction of value-added tax (VAT) in 2002.	Relatively durable, with renewed efforts in 2001–02. Adjustment less than planned (7.4 percent of GDP vs. 11 percent) and concentrated on spending in 1998, as lower revenue gains reflected weak growth. Arrears increased by 2.3 percent of GDP. Slippage in 2000 by 6 percent of GDP reflected elections, oil prices, and conflict in southern Lebanon. Primary balance improved by 9.2 percent of GDP in 2001–02 through spending cuts and new VAT.
Lithuania 1999–2003	Deficit was reduced as targeted through larger expenditure cuts; revenues declined by 1.4 percent of GDP. Spending cuts of 6.7 percent of GDP focused on household transfers (3.1 percent), goods and services (1.3 percent), wages (0.6 percent), and net lending (1.7 percent). Arrears reduced by 0.9 percent of GDP.	Durable. Further adjustment in 2001 and 2002 by 0.8 percent of GDP in each year. Revenue decline continued; spending cuts concentrated on the wage bill and household transfers. Public debt reduced. Lower interest payments and initiation of grants from the EU helped defray increased capital spending from 2002.
New Zealand 1983–88	The primary balance was improved by 10½ percentage points of GDP, 4.2 percentage points from revenue measures and 6.3 percentage points from spending cuts. A shortfall of 1.5 percent of GDP relative to adjustment targets was experienced in the second year.	Durable. Primary surpluses were maintained through the 1990s, compared with sizable pre-adjustment deficits. Public debt reduced from a peak of 82 percent of GDP in 1987 to 31 percent in 2001. Continued reduction in government in the 1990s, with revenues lower by 10.3 percent of GDP and spending reduced by 8.5 percent of GDP.

Table A3.3 *(concluded)*

Episode	Fiscal Impact	Durability of Fiscal Impact
Nigeria 1990–2000	Data shortcomings limit assessment, but the primary balance improved by 9 percent of GDP during 1995–97, compared with 1993–94. Non-oil primary balance to non-oil GDP improved by 20 percentage points. Primary balance deteriorated in 1998, reflecting lower oil prices and production. With price and production increases in 1999–2000, the primary balance improved, although the non-oil primary balance deteriorated by 5 percentage points.	Not durable. Fiscal balances deteriorated with the oil price decline in 1998. Wage increases introduced without supporting civil service reforms, and fiscal federalism changes introduced in 1999 have weakened fiscal policy management.
Russia 1999–2002	The federal balance improved from a deficit of 6 percent of GDP in 1998 to surpluses in 2000–02. Revenues increased by 6.7 percentage points of GDP, due largely to the recovery of oil prices and the ruble depreciation. Revenues were helped by tax reforms introduced in 1999 and 2001 (introduction of new oil taxes, rationalization of tax structure). The interest bill was reduced sharply with the default, and the primary balance improved by 8 percent of GDP to a surplus of over 5 percent in 2000–02.	Durable, with support of continued high oil prices and improved expenditure control, which contributed to the reduction of arrears. The non-oil primary deficit improved from 6.0 percent of GDP in 1998 to 0.4 in 2000, but weakened to 4.9 percent of GDP by 2002.
South Africa 1993–2001	The overall deficit was reduced by 6½ percent of GDP from 1992/93 to 2002/03. Revenue gains accounted for 3 percentage points, while spending cuts amounted to 3½ percent of GDP. A strengthening of the primary balance by 6½ percentage points of GDP took place through 1999/2000. With a decline in the interest bill thereafter, social and capital spending were increased.	Durable. The overall deficit decreased in every year from 1992/93 to 2002/03, notwithstanding the authorities' efforts in recent years to increase social spending and provide tax relief. Public debt was reduced by 10 percentage points of GDP from a peak of 48 percent in 1997/98.
Zambia 1989–94	The overall balance improved by 9.6 percentage points of GDP from 1988 to 1992, and the primary balance improved by nearly 15 percent of GDP. Much of the improvement reflected a reinitiation of donor grants from 1991. Tax revenues increased by 4.3 percent of GDP during 1989–90, before slipping.	Not durable. Although the cash fiscal balance improved, the strengthening largely reflected increases in external assistance, while expenditure arrears increased. Little progress was made in privatization, in reducing maize subsidies, or in civil service reform, while there was overspending on the wage bill. The adjustment was undermined by drought in 1992.

Sources: Country authorities; and IMF staff reports.

Table A3.4. Key Fiscal Structural Reforms and Subnational Adjustments

Episode	Key Fiscal Structural Reforms	Subnational Adjustments
Brazil 1999–2003	Well-established legal framework for developing, implementing, and monitoring the annual budget law, supported by the Fiscal Responsibility Law, the constitutional provisions on public financial management in general, the multiyear plan, and the Budget Guidelines Law, which sets targets for three years ahead on a rolling basis. Tax and pension reform. Improvements in revenue administration. Privatization and increased commercial orientation of public enterprises.	Debt restructuring agreements between the federal government and subnational governments and legislation limiting personnel expenditures and debt at all levels of government paved the way for a comprehensive Fiscal Responsibility Law supporting fiscal prudence and rules-based fiscal policy. The primary balance of subnational governments improved from a deficit of ½ percent of GDP in 1998 to a surplus of nearly 1 percent of GDP in 2003, mainly on the basis of higher revenues.
Canada 1993–2000	Introduction of medium-term budget framework; shift to block transfers; tax reforms (personal income tax (PIT), corporate income tax (CIT) base broadening, and rate reductions); pension reform; unemployment insurance reform.	Cuts in the provincial wage bill, capital spending, and municipal transfers of 1.7 percent of GDP in 1993/94. Provinces raised education and health fees and excises and broadened the CIT base. Ontario and Quebec eliminated deficits in the late 1990s (3 percent of provincial GDP).
Côte d'Ivoire 1993–2000	Creation of a large taxpayer unit and improved customs administration.	
Finland 1992–2000	Introduction of medium-term budget framework; shift to block transfers; tax reform (PIT, CIT base broadening, and rate reductions); pension reform.	2.3 percent of GDP adjustment during 1993–94, with cuts in capital spending (1 percent) and current spending (1 percent, largely employment and wages) and a property tax increase (0.4 percent).
Jamaica 1998–2001	2000 Staff Monitored Program (SMP) targeted cost recovery in health and education and rationalization of safety net; 2002 SMP targeted enterprise reforms.	
Lebanon 1998–2002	Improved expenditure forecasting and tax and customs administration reforms. Limited expenditure management reforms to address carryover of unused funds.	Municipal transfers were not made during 1993–96 by the central government. An agreement was reached in 2000 to provide a one-time payment in 2003.
Lithuania 1999–2003	Strengthened treasury and commitment controls; fiscal reserve fund; organic budget law and medium-term framework; consolidation of extrabudgetary funds.	Municipal expenditure arrears were to be eliminated. Formulas introduced for municipal spending requirements, central government transfers, and local borrowing.
New Zealand 1983–88	Introduction of medium-term budget framework; new VAT; PIT and CIT base broadening and rate reductions; enterprise privatization; pension reforms.	
Nigeria 1990–2000		Constitutional reforms in 1999 devolved greater responsibilities to subnationals, although few mechanisms for coordination established.
Russia 1995–98	Efforts to improve tax policy and administration and public expenditure management and control.	Expenditure management weaknesses among subnational governments contributed to arrears.
Russia 1999–2002	Introduction of new oil taxes (including export tariff and simplified oil extraction tax); improved expenditure control and management, together with centralization of taxes to the federal government.	Transfers to regions cut by 1½ percent of GDP, and regional spending cut by 5 percent of GDP, with focus on social spending.
South Africa 1993–2001	Base broadening and lower rates for income taxes; revenue administration reforms; medium-term budget framework; improved expenditure planning and management, accounting and reporting, and oversight.	Strengthening of provincial finances, improvements in treasury control, centralization of personnel spending, revenue sharing formula, expenditure norms.
Zambia 1989–94	Civil service reforms planned, but not fully implemented; consolidation of revenue administration.	

Sources: Country authorities; and IMF staff reports.

Table A3.5. Macroeconomic Impact of Large Fiscal Adjustment

Episode	Macroeconomic Impact of Large Fiscal Adjustment
Brazil 1999–2003	Initial growth spurt in 2000, followed by years of sluggish growth performance, affected by external shocks, domestic politics, and an energy crisis in 2001. Successful transition to a floating exchange regime after 1999, with relatively low inflation and strengthening of the financial system. Significant turnaround in the external current account and reduction in external vulnerabilities. Fiscal vulnerabilities remain, despite improvements in the most recent period, particularly related to (1) still-high public net debt, at short maturity and highly sensitive to interest rate and exchange rate movements; (2) significant budget rigidities; (3) large pension system imbalances; (4) constrained public investment; and (5) cumbersome tax system.
Canada 1993–2000	Initial growth spurt, led by exports and investment, followed by two years of slower growth, as adjustment was implemented. Sustained high growth followed, with low inflation. Improved current account, led by improved public savings, sharply reduced net foreign debt.
Côte d'Ivoire 1993–2000	Performance improved in the immediate aftermath of the CFA franc devaluation, with GDP growth of over 7 percent in 1995–96, 5.7 percent in 1997, and 4.8 percent in 1998. Inflation increased in 1994, but returned to low single-digit levels by 1996. Governance issues (fraud and misappropriation of aid), terms-of-trade deterioration, and political tensions culminating in a December 1999 coup contributed to weaker performance after 1999.
Finland 1992–2000	Continued recession in 1992–93 but sharp reduction in inflation and the current account deficit. From 1994, strong investment and export-led growth, low inflation, and current account surplus. Sharp growth of information and computer technology sector in mid- and late 1990s, led by Nokia, contributed to increased fiscal revenues. Net public external debt eliminated by 2002.
Jamaica 1998–2001	Modest GDP growth of 1 percent per year resumed in 2000–01, following three years of decline. Inflation remained subdued, and foreign reserves were boosted by high interest rates and remittances. Unemployment remained high, and the current account deficit widened in 2000/01 and 2001/02.
Lebanon 1998–2002	Cuts in public investment dampened activity, but possibly by less than without adjustment. Growth in 1999–2000 was hampered by high interest rates and exchange rate appreciation. Incipient recovery in 2001–02 was stalled by gradual loss of market confidence, followed by strong fiscal adjustment.
Lithuania 1999–2003	Recovery began in 2000, initially led by reorientation of exports to central and western Europe. Unemployment rose sharply in 2000–01. Low wage growth and labor market reforms helped competitiveness, and the current account deficit improved by 6.4 percent of GDP in 2000–01. Recovery of domestic demand and investment led to accelerating growth from 2001. Low inflation continued, and the currency board was repegged to the euro in 2002.
New Zealand 1983–88	After adjustment and lifting of trade and price controls, a period of volatile growth and high inflation was experienced. Tight monetary and fiscal policy contributed to stagnation for several years but helped reduce inflation and the current account deficit.
Nigeria 1990–2000	Fiscal adjustment in 1995–97 contributed to higher foreign exchange reserves and lower inflation of less than 10 percent annually in 1997–99. Adjustment had little impact on growth performance, which was affected more by changes in oil production.
Russia 1995–98	Inflation was reduced sharply during 1995–98 through adjustment and exchange rate stability. Adjustment was made more difficult by the complex ongoing transition and a decline of oil prices in 1998. Debt default in August 1998 led to a sharp depreciation of the ruble.
Russia 1999–2002	Growth improved with higher oil prices and increased net exports during 1999–2000, aided by substantial real depreciation of the ruble. Inflation reduced from 85 percent in 1999 to 20 percent in 2000–01. Investment recovered strongly from 2000.
South Africa 1993–2001	Reflecting post-apartheid structural reforms and fiscal adjustment, economic performance improved, with lower inflation and higher growth during 1994–2002 (2.8 percent per year), as compared with 1985–93 (0.6 percent). Savings and investment rates remained low, however, and unemployment high. Concerns have arisen over the impacts of HIV/AIDS.
Zambia 1989–94	With a lower deficit and less domestic financing, inflation was reduced from 150 percent in 1989 to 50 percent in 1994, and the current account balance improved. A substantial depreciation caused the public debt ratio to increase sharply from 1990.

Sources: Country authorities; and IMF staff reports.

Table A3.6. Role of the IMF

Episode	Role of the IMF During Adjustment Episode
Brazil 1999–2003	Stand-By Arrangements (end-1998–2001; 2001–02; 2002–March 2005). Technical assistance (TA) from Monetary and Financial Systems Department (MFD), Fiscal Affairs Department (FAD), and Statistics (STA) Department.
Canada 1993–2000	Surveillance
Côte d'Ivoire 1993–2000	Two arrangements under the Enhanced Structural Adjustment Facility (ESAF) (1994–96, 1998–2000) TA.
Finland 1992–2000	Surveillance
Jamaica 1998–2001	Policy consultations, Staff Monitored Programs (SMPs) in 2000 and 2002; TA in banking supervision and restructuring.
Lebanon 1998–2002	TA in introduction of the value-added tax (VAT), reforms to customs tariffs and the income tax, tax administration, and expenditure management.
Lithuania 1999–2003	Precautionary Stand-By Arrangements in March 2000 and August 2001; TA in treasury operations, reserve fund, and tax policy.
New Zealand 1983–88	Surveillance
Nigeria 1990–2000	Stand-By Arrangement agreed following the transition to democratic rule.
Russia 1995–98	Stand-By Arrangement in 1995; arrangement under the Extended Fund Facility in 1996; extensive program of TA.
Russia 1999–2002	Stand-By Arrangement in July 1999 as a precondition for rescheduling debt of Paris (1999) and London (2000) Clubs; extensive TA continued.
South Africa 1993–2001	Arrangement under the Compensatory and Contingency Financing Facility (CCFF) in 1993; surveillance thereafter.
Zambia 1989–94	Rights accumulation program in 1991; TA on budget execution; World Bank TA on civil service reforms and privatization.

Sources: Country authorities; and IMF staff reports.

Appendix IV   Econometric Methodology

The duration of fiscal consolidation can be expressed by a hazard function. A hazard function measures the probability that a fiscal consolidation will end in time period t, provided that the adjustment was still ongoing in the previous period. Mathematically, a "survivor function" can be defined as $S(t) = Pr(T \geq t)$. The corresponding "failure function" then becomes $F(t) = 1 - S(t)$, with a probability density $f(t) = dF(t)/dt$. The hazard function, $h(t)$, can then be written as:

$$h(t) = \frac{f(t)}{S(t)}. \tag{1}$$

The unconditional hazard function can be used to compare consolidation exit rates across groups of similar countries. To assess factors underlying the sustainability of fiscal consolidation, a model is required that allows for dependence of the hazard function on explanatory variables. A commonly used model of proportional hazard assumes that the conditional probability that consolidation will end is rescaled by a function g of several covariates:

$$h(t, X) = h_0(t) * g(X). \tag{2}$$

The model is estimated using either semiparametric or parametric techniques. Semiparametric estimation (following Cox, 1972) requires no specific functional form for the baseline hazard function $h_0(t)$, and sets $g(X) = \exp(X'\beta)$. Parametric estimation imposes a specific functional form for the baseline hazard, which provides for more efficient estimation, if a priori information is available about the shape of the hazard function. Parametric estimation also sets $g(X) = \exp(X'\beta)$. The most commonly assumed functional form is Weibull:

$$h_0(t) = pt^{p-1} \exp(\beta_0). \tag{3}$$

The Weibull functional form allows one to test whether there is positive duration dependence or "consolidation fatigue." This occurs when $p > 1$.

Once estimated, several tests may be used to assess the validity of the proportional hazard assumption and, more generally, the functional form and fit of the model. To test the validity of the proportional hazard assumption, one may employ a generalized version of the Grambsh-Therneau test. For goodness of fit, one may use the Hosmer and Lemeshow analysis of Cox-Snell residuals.

Appendix V   Macroeconomic Impact of Fiscal Adjustment

Figure A5.1. Event Studies: Key Macroeconomic Indicators
(Annual percentage change, unless indicated otherwise)

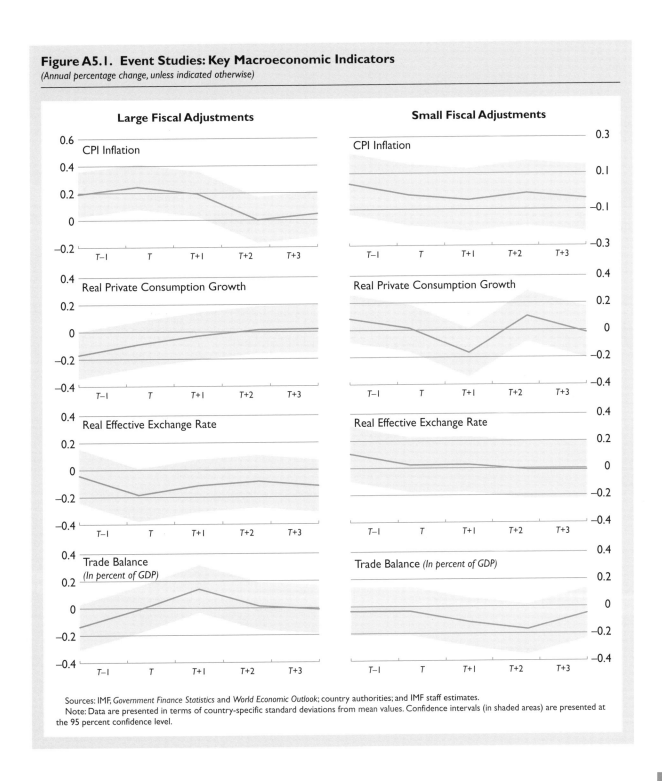

Sources: IMF, *Government Finance Statistics* and *World Economic Outlook*; country authorities; and IMF staff estimates.
Note: Data are presented in terms of country-specific standard deviations from mean values. Confidence intervals (in shaded areas) are presented at the 95 percent confidence level.

Figure A5.2. Event Studies: CPI Inflation and Real Private Consumption Growth
(Annual percentage change)

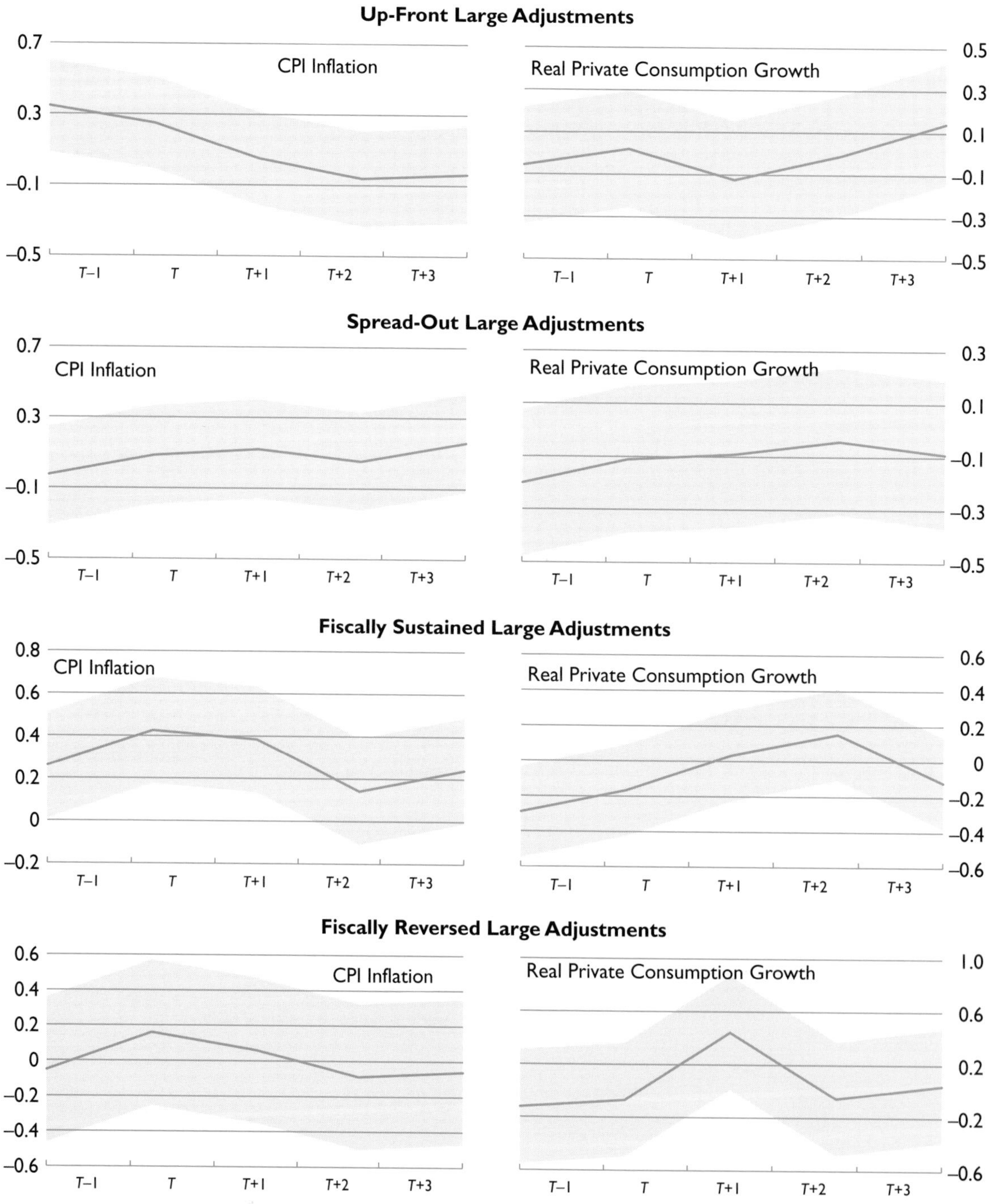

Sources: IMF, *Government Finance Statistics* and *World Economic Outlook*; country authorities; and IMF staff estimates.
Note: Data are presented in terms of country-specific standard deviations from mean values. Confidence intervals (in shaded areas) are presented at the 95 percent confidence level.

Figure A5.3. Event Studies: Key External Indicators

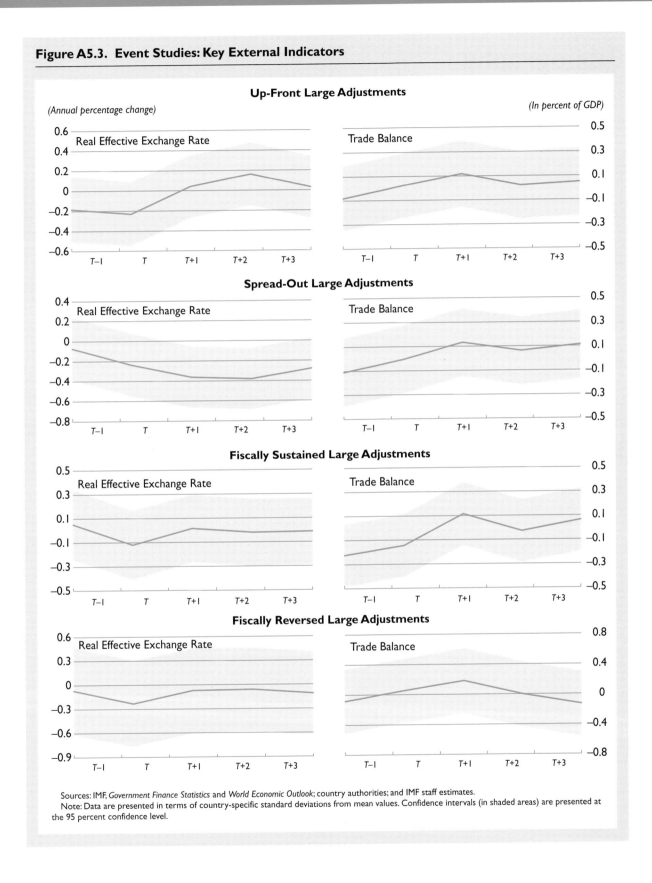

Sources: IMF, *Government Finance Statistics* and *World Economic Outlook*; country authorities; and IMF staff estimates.
Note: Data are presented in terms of country-specific standard deviations from mean values. Confidence intervals (in shaded areas) are presented at the 95 percent confidence level.

Bibliography

Abed, George T., Liam Ebrill, Sanjeev Gupta, Benedict Clements, Ronald McMorran, Anthony Pellechio, Jerald Schiff, and Marijn Verhoeven, 1998, *Fiscal Reforms in Low-Income Countries: Experience Under IMF-Supported Programs,* IMF Occasional Paper No. 160 (Washington: International Monetary Fund).

Adam, Christopher, and David Bevan, 2004, "Staying the Course: Maintaining Fiscal Control in Developing Countries," in *Brookings Trade Forum, 2003,* ed. by Susan Collins and Dani Rodrik (Washington: Brookings Institution).

Alesina, Alberto, and Silvia Ardagna, 1998, "Tales of Fiscal Adjustment," *Economic Policy,* Vol. 13, No. 27, pp. 487–545.

Alesina, Alberto, and Allan Drazen, 1991, "Why Are Stabilizations Delayed?" *American Economic Review,* Vol. 81, pp. 1170–88.

Alesina, Alberto, and Roberto Perotti, 1996, "Fiscal Adjustments in OECD Countries: Composition and Macroeconomic Effects," NBER Working Paper No. 5730 (Cambridge, Massachusetts: National Bureau of Economic Research).

———, and José Tavares, 1998, "The Political Economy of Fiscal Adjustments," *Brookings Papers on Economic Activity: 1,* Brookings Institution.

Cox, D.R., 1972, "Regression Models and Life Tables," *Journal of the Royal Statistical Society,* Series B, Vol. 34, No. 2, pp. 187–202.

Giavazzi, Francesco, Tullio Jappelli, and Marco Pagano, 2000, "Searching for Non-Linear Effects of Fiscal Policy: Evidence from Industrial and Developing Countries," *European Economic Review,* Vol. 44, No. 7, pp. 1259–89.

Giavazzi, Francesco, and Marco Pagano, 1990, "Can Severe Fiscal Contractions Be Expansionary? Tales of Two Small European Countries," NBER Working Paper No. 3372 (Cambridge, Massachusetts: National Bureau of Economic Research).

Goldsbrough, David, Sharmini Coorey, Louis Dicks-Mireaux, Balazs Horvath, Kalpana Kochhar, Mauro Mecagni, Erik Offerdal, and Jianping Zhou, 1996, *Reinvigorating Growth in Developing Countries: Lessons from Adjustment Policies in Eight Economies,* IMF Occasional Paper No. 139 (Washington: International Monetary Fund).

Gupta, Sanjeev, Benedict Clements, Emanuele Baldacci, and Carlos Mulas-Granados, 2004, "The Persistence of Fiscal Adjustment in Developing Countries," *Applied Economics Letters,* Vol. 11, No. 4, pp. 209–12.

———, 2005, "Fiscal Policy, Expenditure Composition, and Growth in Low-Income Countries," *Journal of International Money and Finance,* Vol. 24, No. 3, pp. 441–63.

Han, Aaron, and Jerry A. Hausman, 1990, "Flexible Parametric Estimation of Duration and Competing Risk Models," *Journal of Applied Econometrics,* Vol. 5, No. 1, pp. 1–28.

Hemming, Richard, Michael Kell, and Axel Schimmelpfennig, 2003, *Fiscal Vulnerability and Financial Crises in Emerging Market Economies,* IMF Occasional Paper No. 218 (Washington: International Monetary Fund).

International Monetary Fund, Independent Evaluation Office, 2003a, *Evaluation Report: Fiscal Adjustment in IMF-Supported Programs* (Washington).

———, 2003b, *IMF and Recent Capital Account Crises: Indonesia, Korea, Brazil* (Washington).

———, 2004, *The IMF and Argentina, 1991–2001* (Washington).

Mackenzie, G.A., David W.H. Orsmond, and Philip R. Gerson, 1997, *The Composition of Fiscal Adjustment and Growth: Lessons from Fiscal Reforms in Eight Economies,* IMF Occasional Paper No. 149 (Washington: International Monetary Fund).

McDermott, C. John, and Robert F. Wescott, 1996, "An Empirical Analysis of Fiscal Adjustments," IMF Working Paper 96/59 (Washington: International Monetary Fund).

Narendranathan, Wiji, and Mark B. Stewart, 1993, "Modelling the Probability of Leaving Unemployment: Competing Risks Models with Flexible Base-Line Hazards," *Applied Statistics,* Vol. 42, No. 1, pp. 63–83.

Perotti, Roberto, 1999, "Fiscal Policy in Good Times and Bad," *Quarterly Journal of Economics,* Vol. 114, No. 4 (November), pp. 1399–1436.

Von Hagen, Jürgen, Andrew Hughes Hallet, and Rolf Strauch, 2001, "Budgetary Consolidation in EMU," *European Economy—Economic Papers,* No. 148 (Brussels: Commission of the European Communities, Directorate-General for Economic and Financial Affairs, March).

Recent Occasional Papers of the International Monetary Fund

246. Experience with Large Fiscal Adjustments, by George C. Tsibouris, Mark A. Horton, Mark J. Flanagan, and Wojciech S. Maliszewski. 2006.

245. Budget System Reform in Emerging Economies: The Challenges and the Reform Agenda, by Jack Diamond. 2006.

244. Monetary Policy Implementation at Different Stages of Market Development, by a staff team led by Bernard J. Laurens. 2005.

243. Central America: Global Integration and Regional Cooperation, edited by Markus Rodlauer and Alfred Schipke. 2005.

242. Turkey at the Crossroads: From Crisis Resolution to EU Accession, by a staff team led by Reza Moghadam. 2005.

241. The Design of IMF-Supported Programs, by Atish Ghosh, Charis Christofides, Jun Kim, Laura Papi, Uma Ramakrishnan, Alun Thomas, and Juan Zalduendo. 2005.

240. Debt-Related Vulnerabilities and Financial Crises: An Application of the Balance Sheet Approach to Emerging Market Countries, by Christoph Rosenberg, Ioannis Halikias, Brett House, Christian Keller, Jens Nystedt, Alexander Pitt, and Brad Setser. 2005.

239. GEM: A New International Macroeconomic Model, by Tamim Bayoumi, with assistance from Douglas Laxton, Hamid Faruqee, Benjamin Hunt, Philippe Karam, Jaewoo Lee, Alessandro Rebucci, and Ivan Tchakarov. 2004.

238. Stabilization and Reforms in Latin America: A Macroeconomic Perspective on the Experience Since the Early 1990s, by Anoop Singh, Agnès Belaisch, Charles Collyns, Paula De Masi, Reva Krieger, Guy Meredith, and Robert Rennhack. 2005.

237. Sovereign Debt Structure for Crisis Prevention, by Eduardo Borensztein, Marcos Chamon, Olivier Jeanne, Paolo Mauro, and Jeromin Zettelmeyer. 2004.

236. Lessons from the Crisis in Argentina, by Christina Daseking, Atish R. Ghosh, Alun Thomas, and Timothy Lane. 2004.

235. A New Look at Exchange Rate Volatility and Trade Flows, by Peter B. Clark, Natalia Tamirisa, and Shang-Jin Wei, with Azim Sadikov and Li Zeng. 2004.

234. Adopting the Euro in Central Europe: Challenges of the Next Step in European Integration, by Susan M. Schadler, Paulo F. Drummond, Louis Kuijs, Zuzana Murgasova, and Rachel N. van Elkan. 2004.

233. Germany's Three-Pillar Banking System: Cross-Country Perspectives in Europe, by Allan Brunner, Jörg Decressin, Daniel Hardy, and Beata Kudela. 2004.

232. China's Growth and Integration into the World Economy: Prospects and Challenges, edited by Eswar Prasad. 2004.

231. Chile: Policies and Institutions Underpinning Stability and Growth, by Eliot Kalter, Steven Phillips, Marco A. Espinosa-Vega, Rodolfo Luzio, Mauricio Villafuerte, and Manmohan Singh. 2004.

230. Financial Stability in Dollarized Countries, by Anne-Marie Gulde, David Hoelscher, Alain Ize, David Marston, and Gianni De Nicoló. 2004.

229. Evolution and Performance of Exchange Rate Regimes, by Kenneth S. Rogoff, Aasim M. Husain, Ashoka Mody, Robin Brooks, and Nienke Oomes. 2004.

228. Capital Markets and Financial Intermediation in The Baltics, by Alfred Schipke, Christian Beddies, Susan M. George, and Niamh Sheridan. 2004.

227. U.S. Fiscal Policies and Priorities for Long-Run Sustainability, edited by Martin Mühleisen and Christopher Towe 2004.

226. Hong Kong SAR: Meeting the Challenges of Integration with the Mainland, edited by Eswar Prasad, with contributions from Jorge Chan-Lau, Dora Iakova, William Lee, Hong Liang, Ida Liu, Papa N'Diaye, and Tao Wang. 2004.

225. Rules-Based Fiscal Policy in France, Germany, Italy, and Spain, by Teresa Dában, Enrica Detragiache, Gabriel di Bella, Gian Maria Milesi-Ferretti, and Steven Symansky. 2003.

224. Managing Systemic Banking Crises, by a staff team led by David S. Hoelscher and Marc Quintyn. 2003.

223. Monetary Union Among Member Countries of the Gulf Cooperation Council, by a staff team led by Ugo Fasano. 2003.

222. Informal Funds Transfer Systems: An Analysis of the Informal Hawala System, by Mohammed El Qorchi, Samuel Munzele Maimbo, and John F. Wilson. 2003.

221. Deflation: Determinants, Risks, and Policy Options, by Manmohan S. Kumar. 2003.

220. Effects of Financial Globalization on Developing Countries: Some Empirical Evidence, by Eswar S. Prasad, Kenneth Rogoff, Shang-Jin Wei, and Ayhan Kose. 2003.

219. Economic Policy in a Highly Dollarized Economy: The Case of Cambodia, by Mario de Zamaroczy and Sopanha Sa. 2003.

218. Fiscal Vulnerability and Financial Crises in Emerging Market Economies, by Richard Hemming, Michael Kell, and Axel Schimmelpfennig. 2003.

217. Managing Financial Crises: Recent Experience and Lessons for Latin America, edited by Charles Collyns and G. Russell Kincaid. 2003.

216. Is the PRGF Living Up to Expectations?—An Assessment of Program Design, by Sanjeev Gupta, Mark Plant, Benedict Clements, Thomas Dorsey, Emanuele Baldacci, Gabriela Inchauste, Shamsuddin Tareq, and Nita Thacker. 2002.

215. Improving Large Taxpayers' Compliance: A Review of Country Experience, by Katherine Baer. 2002.

214. Advanced Country Experiences with Capital Account Liberalization, by Age Bakker and Bryan Chapple. 2002.

213. The Baltic Countries: Medium-Term Fiscal Issues Related to EU and NATO Accession, by Johannes Mueller, Christian Beddies, Robert Burgess, Vitali Kramarenko, and Joannes Mongardini. 2002.

212. Financial Soundness Indicators: Analytical Aspects and Country Practices, by V. Sundararajan, Charles Enoch, Armida San José, Paul Hilbers, Russell Krueger, Marina Moretti, and Graham Slack. 2002.

211. Capital Account Liberalization and Financial Sector Stability, by a staff team led by Shogo Ishii and Karl Habermeier. 2002.

210. IMF-Supported Programs in Capital Account Crises, by Atish Ghosh, Timothy Lane, Marianne Schulze-Ghattas, Aleš Bulíř, Javier Hamann, and Alex Mourmouras. 2002.

209. Methodology for Current Account and Exchange Rate Assessments, by Peter Isard, Hamid Faruqee, G. Russell Kincaid, and Martin Fetherston. 2001.

208. Yemen in the 1990s: From Unification to Economic Reform, by Klaus Enders, Sherwyn Williams, Nada Choueiri, Yuri Sobolev, and Jan Walliser. 2001.

207. Malaysia: From Crisis to Recovery, by Kanitta Meesook, Il Houng Lee, Olin Liu, Yougesh Khatri, Natalia Tamirisa, Michael Moore, and Mark H. Krysl. 2001.

206. The Dominican Republic: Stabilization, Structural Reform, and Economic Growth, by a staff team led by Philip Young comprising Alessandro Giustiniani, Werner C. Keller, and Randa E. Sab and others. 2001.

205. Stabilization and Savings Funds for Nonrenewable Resources, by Jeffrey Davis, Rolando Ossowski, James Daniel, and Steven Barnett. 2001.

204. Monetary Union in West Africa (ECOWAS): Is It Desirable and How Could It Be Achieved? by Paul Masson and Catherine Pattillo. 2001.

203. Modern Banking and OTC Derivatives Markets: The Transformation of Global Finance and Its Implications for Systemic Risk, by Garry J. Schinasi, R. Sean Craig, Burkhard Drees, and Charles Kramer. 2000.

202. Adopting Inflation Targeting: Practical Issues for Emerging Market Countries, by Andrea Schaechter, Mark R. Stone, and Mark Zelmer. 2000.

Note: For information on the titles and availability of Occasional Papers not listed, please consult the IMF's *Publications Catalog* or contact IMF Publication Services.